Reformation of War, Part 1

J.F.C. Fuller

This is a curated and comprehensive collection of the most important works covering matters related to national security, diplomacy, defense, war, strategy, and tactics. The collection spans centuries of thought and experience, and includes the latest analysis of international threats, both conventional and asymmetric. It also includes riveting first person accounts of historic battles and wars.

Some of the books in this Series are reproductions of historical works preserved by some of the leading libraries in the world. As with any reproduction of a historical artifact, some of these books contain missing or blurred pages, poor pictures, errant marks, etc. We believe these books are essential to this collection and the study of war, and have therefore brought them back into print, despite these imperfections.

We hope you enjoy the unmatched breadth and depth of this collection, from the historical to the just-published works.

The Reformation of War

THE REFORMATION OF WAR.

By Col. J. F. C. Fuller, D.S.O.

Author of "Tanks in the Great War," "Training Soldiers for War," etc. :: :: :: :: :: ::

The Spirit of Progress: "Halt! Who goes there?"
The Spirit of Mankind: "War!"
The Spirit of Progress: "Pass, War, all's well!"

NEW YORK:

E. P. DUTTON AND COMPANY

681, FIFTH AVENUE

1923

Printed in Great Britain

DEDICATE THIS BOOK

TO THE

𝔘𝔫𝔨𝔫𝔬𝔴𝔫 𝔚𝔞𝔯𝔯𝔦𝔬𝔯

IN WHOSE BROKEN BODY

LIVES THE MEMORY OF A MILLION BRITISH DEAD

WHO FEAR NOT FORGETFULNESS

IF THROUGH THEIR SACRIFICE

WAR MAY BE ENNOBLED AND REFORMED

PREFACE

" Big Mars seems bankrupt in their beggar'd host,
 And faintly through a rusty beaver peeps :
 The horsemen sit like fixed candlesticks,
 With torch-staves in their hand. . . ."

King Henry V., IV. ii. 43.

" O ! now doth Death line his dead chaps with steel ;
 The swords of soldiers are his teeth, his fangs ;
 And now he feasts, mousing the flesh of man."

King John, II. i. 351.

ALAS ! that I should have been born in the last quarter of the nineteenth century, for, had this event taken place a hundred years earlier, I should have been spared many troubles, including the writing of this book. In those days warfare was so simple, and, by education, I ought to be a follower of Major Gahagan— seeing that I am an admirer of his " tremendous adventures."

" On they came ; my guns and men were ready for them. You will ask how my pieces were loaded ? I answer, that though my garrison were without food, I knew my duty as an officer, and *had put the two Dutch cheeses into the two guns, and had crammed the contents of a bottle of olives into each swivel.*

" They advanced—whish went one of the Dutch cheeses, bang went the other ! Alas, they did little execution. In their first contact with an opposing body, they certainly floored it, but they became at once like so much Welsh rabbit, and did no execution beyond the man whom they struck down.

" ' Hogree, pogree, wongree-fum ' (praise to Allah and the forty-nine Imaums !) shouted out the ferocious Loll Mahommed when he saw the failure of my shot. ' Onward, sons of the Prophet ! The infidel has no more ammunition. A hundred thousand lakhs of rupees to the man who brings me Gahagan's head ! '

" I gave one thought to my blessed, my beautiful Belinda, and then, stepping into the front, took down one of the swivels. A

7

shower of matchlock balls came whizzing round my head. I did not heed them.

"I took the swivel and aimed coolly. Loll Mahommed, his palanquin and his men, were now not above two hundred yards from the fort. Loll was straight before me, gesticulating and shouting to his men. I fired—bang ! ! !

"I aimed so true that *one hundred and seventeen best Spanish olives were lodged in a lump in the face of the unhappy Loll Mahommed.* The wretch, uttering a yell the most hideous and unearthly I ever heard, fell back dead. The frightened bearers flung down the palanquin and ran. The whole host ran as one man, their screams might be heard for leagues. '*Tomasha, tomasha,*' they cried, 'it is enchantment.' Away they fled, and the victory a third time was ours. Soon as the fight was done, I flew back to my Belinda. . . ."

In his heart of hearts, who would not be a traditional soldier, a Gahagan with his fair Belinda ? And yet, through some trick in my nature, I intend to inquire into the probabilities of future warfare in place of examining the tactics of the Ahmednuggar Irregulars. I admit it is a surprising thing to do, seeing that I have successfully passed all my military examinations and some even with distinction ; but the ways of man are inscrutable, so I will say no more.

I intend inquiring into the nature of future warfare, not because I love war or hate war, but because I believe that war is of the inevitable, and that the greatest of all heresies and delusions concerning it is to suppose that the Great War of 1914-1918 is the last of all wars. That it may be the last of its kind I full-heartedly agree to, so much so that I believe the nature of the next great war will be totally different from the last ; so different that, even if great nations go to war in 1950, the recent war will appear to those not far distant fighters as a struggle between barbaric hordes, a saurian contest, not mediæval but primæval, archaic, a turmoil, which in the history of the evolution of warfare is more distant from that day than the Marne was from Marathon.

If, after meditating on the views set forth in this book, the reader believes that I am right, even if only partially so, then this book is worth supporting ; if he believes, however, that I am wrong, even if totally so, then this book is worth refuting; for war is a serious problem, and the next war the most serious of all problems: this at least the last war should have taught us. To meditate is not only to think and think again, but to think rightly, logically according to facts, to discover the soul of thought; and this can never be done if our minds are shackled by our sentiments or stamped by our emotions. To anathematize war is to gibber like a fool, and to declare it to be unreasonable, is to twaddle like a pedant. Love is unreasonable and so is madness. All things divine and diabolical are unreasonable, and mixed with clay from out these two unreasoning opposites emerges man, a vibrating mass of unreasoning instincts which will out, and demoniacally so when they are imprisoned. As well attempt to damp down Erebus with a duster as to attempt to control the primitive instincts of man by oath, syllogism, or agreement.

To some, the one unforgivable sin in man is that he is human —a thinking beast, a discontented animal; these believe in original sin. I do not; I believe in original thought and spew out that nauseous mental drug called imitation. I may be a heretic, a military Luther, yet nevertheless I try to accept man as God made him, and not as Mr. Smith would like him to be. Tell me, studious reader, which of us two blasphemes, Smith or I?

Frankly I am critical, not only because I refuse to be led by a halter, but because, in my heart, I have a very warm place for Mr. Smith, who, as Private, Sergeant, Subaltern and General, has been for many years my friend and companion. I have watched him in two long wars struggling against odds, and I have learnt to appreciate his virtues, and his failings, and his indomitable courage. He is a man who possesses such natural pride of birth that, through sheer contempt for others, he refuses to learn or to be defeated. He divides humanity into two classes: Englishmen and niggers, and of the second class some happen to be black and others white. He only condescends to differentiate between these sub-classes by calling the latter dagoes. To him, all white folk, outside his own little islands, are such. From these he has nothing to learn, yet he is tolerant, tolerant as he would be to his dog ; he has, in fact, raised the vice of contempt to a high virtue and on this virtue is the British Empire founded.

Having nothing to learn, through sheer power of domination, he has become the prince of rulers, and through sheer refusal to be defeated by niggers the master of improvisation. He is always there, for the sun never sets on his Empire, but he is never ready. For readiness would presuppose fear, and what has he, as an Englishman, to be afraid of ? He is an incarnation of King Henry V., and every battle he fights is an Agincourt.

Surely, then, it is but folly to disturb his confidence ? It would be so if the world were what it was, but the world has changed and with it has changed the art of war. The jar of science has been fished up from out the deep, and its seal has been broken, and no English contempt for others will coax the Jinn back into his bottle. We must face facts. Courage is still a great virtue, but the power of knowledge is equally great, and because the Englishman lacks this power, through his sheer contempt to learn, and because I, as an Englishman, love my countrymen, therefore I intend to flog Mr. Smith with criticism. Whether I shall succeed in waking him from his self-pride I cannot tell, for his skin is thick, and he sleeps soundly ; but if I can persuade him to turn over in his bed and for a moment look the other way—future-wards, then I shall not be disappointed. He will accuse me of producing a nightmare, and then, through sheer contempt for such things, he will either fall to sleep again, or perhaps he will rise from his couch.

For many years now have I attempted to wake him, and I have written much on war, so much that this book is but a compilation of past writings brought up to date.* Much that I have written I have already scrapped, and much that I write now I shall scrap if I write more, for knowledge is an ever changing power. The man who never changes his mind, has mineralized his intellect. He is but a walking stone ; he may be shale or Aberdeen granite, it matters not, for dynamite will shatter him,

* In the Appendix will be found a list of these. I have not quoted them in the text as in most cases the wording has been changed.

and it is with dynamite I intend to work. Yet this does not prohibit the discovery of a still more powerful explosive, and, if any of my readers can present me with one, I will accept it, for knowledge to be strong, must be free. To shackle it is, in my humble opinion, to sin against God, for His highest gift to us is intellect.

In this book I do not intend to enter deeply into the biology of war, but in Chapter I. I will briefly examine this subject, for there is such a condition as this, and so little is it understood that even to-day, in this age of scientific thought, there are still many among us who fondly delude themselves into believing that disarmament and words can abolish war. " Take away our weapons and we still have our fists, our teeth and our nails," shriek human instincts ; " and as for words. . . ." the answer is all but lost in a derisive laugh, " we will force you to eat them and then we will eat you. . . . Think you that we can be measured by foot rule and square ? Out fool, our road is freedom ; the direction of our energy you may control, but the onrush of our flight you will never stay."

To those who thus believe, this book may assist them to prepare for war and so lessen, if only for themselves, its catastrophies. To those who do not, then may this book assist them to attack war. I write for both, for those whom I believe to be wise and for those whom I believe to be foolish, for my object is to induce all conditions of men not only to talk of war but to think of war. Thus and thus only shall we learn how to understand war, especially the nature of the next war ; thus shall we learn how to enhance the virtues of war and how to lessen its vices, and, above all, how to fend war off until mankind has recovered from the recent turmoil, and not only recovered but has replaced the civilization then shattered by a nobler human edifice. Without war there would be no driving out of the money-lenders from the temple of human existence. Without it, customs, interests and prejudices would rot and putrefy, and mankind would be slowly asphyxiated by the stench of his own corruption. The Great War, economically, may have been a disaster, yet the sufferings caused by it were the birth-pangs of a new dispensation. Every gain demands a sacrifice, not even a child can be born into this world without the agony of one poor soul, the least offending of all—its mother.

That the ideas set forth in this book will be generally accepted by soldiers I more than doubt. As a soldier I am a heretic. I am a heretic because I have torn up the Old Testament of War and in this book have attempted to replace it by the first pages of a new one. Novelty is a mental laxative which is not tolerated by the military monk. Reader, if you doubt me, then turn to history. Every military invention of note has either been opposed or attributed to the Devil—gunpowder, cannon, naval armour, rams, rifles, breech-loading guns, gas and tanks have all been opposed by the military hierarchy of their day. But they *are* devilish say you; then I answer: "Fool, hold your tongue," for you who are not soldiers are mentally just as constipated. Was it not a civilian who brought a bill before the British Parliament "to prevent the effeminacy of men riding in coaches" at the time when coaches were struggling into existence, and yet others who decried the steamship, locomotive and motor-car. Nearly every great discovery has been opposed—chloroform, vaccination, the law of evolution, salvarsan, auto-suggestion, and so might be added example to example. Yet opposition has had its value; it has forced the new idea to struggle for its existence, and in this struggle has the new idea grown strong, and as it gains strength so does the old idea compromise, knuckle under and, eventually, disappear. Every pioneer is somewhat of a martyr, and every martyr somewhat of a firebrand who kills with ridicule as well as with reason.

I have not written this book for military monks, but for civilians, who pay for their alchemy and mysteries. In war there is nothing mysterious, for it is the most common-sense of all the sciences, and this I will show in Chapter II. If it possess a mystery, then that mystery is unprogressiveness, for it is a mystery that, in a profession which may, at any moment, demand the risk of danger and death, men are to be found willing to base

their work on the campaigns of Waterloo and Sedan when the
only possible war which confronts them is the next one.

In Chapter III. I will examine the ethical side of war, for without a full understanding of this side can there be no debrutalization
of the art.   In Chapter IV. I will show what price the nations of
Europe paid for copying the past, and then in Chapter V. how out
of folly blossomed wisdom ; how it was discovered that science
was the backbone of victory, science which since 1870 had advanced like a giant in seven-league boots while soldiers were
forming fours and practising the goose-step.

In Chapters VI., VII., VIII. and IX., I will deal with future
warfare from a general standpoint, setting before the reader
a series of possible pictures rather than a mass of probable
detail, so that, from the general panorama, he may carry away
with him an idea of the tendencies of war.

I will show that gas can be made the most humane of weapons ; that the aeroplane will create a new line of attack ;
that the tank is as superior to present-day troops as modern
battleships are to galleys and galleons. I will examine the
purposes of fleets and speculate on their strategy and tactics
in the future, and show that though the principles of war do not
change, their correct application is subject to circumstances.

In writing this book it was first my intention only to deal
with the question of future great wars, but, in thinking this
matter over, I have considered it as well to add a chapter,
Chapter X., on small wars and internal security, as these problems
are those which immediately concern us in our great problem
of Imperial defence. As this question is one which is ever
latent and from which we are never free, I have dealt more
with present than with future possibilities, but have again
attempted to avoid much detail.

In the remaining three Chapters—XI., XII. and XIII., I have
sketched the groundwork of reformation. Taking the body
of man as my prototype, I have outlined the machinery of
reorganization. In Chapter XI. I have attempted to create a
military brain, an organ which can control the entire defence

Preface

forces of the nation. In Chapter XII. I have attempted to fashion a mould in which a new army can be cast, and in Chapter XIII. I have attempted to show that beyond the mind and body of man stands society, and so also with the defence forces, beyond these lies the nation, and that between these two must there be harmony; consequently without national reform can there be no true military reform, for the reform of both is interdependent.

Now that it is written and I can look back on this book, it appears to me that I have not so much set out to discover a new world as to uncover an old one: " The thing that hath been, it is that which shall be ; and that which is done is that which shall be done : and there is no new thing under the sun.''

For the student, let him visit the London Museum and on the top storey he will find in a small room a model of St. James's as it was in 1814. On it he will see rising out of the Green Park a temple. It is called the " Temple of Concord,'' and on the wall he will see a picture of this " pious hope '' which resembles a painted wedding cake surrounded by smoke and fire, and from the inscription on this picture the student will learn that, at midnight of August 1, 1814, London witnessed the celebration of the Great Peace.

The booming of those maroons and the star showers of those rockets have long passed into oblivion, and so has that Temple of Concord. A hundred years later, almost to the minute, Europe was once again flaming with war. What a lesson ! Indeed " there is no new thing under the sun.''

In this book I shall omit much which, were books less expensive to produce, I should have included. Some points I shall repeat again and again, and with a purpose—to drive them home. Traditionalism is the dragon I am out to slay, that servile monster which breathes forth wars of bloodshed and destruction. I will show that the true purpose of war is to create and not to destroy, and that, still to-day, all armies and fleets are spell-bound by the past, and that the nations which support them and pay vast sums for their maintenance, are paying for either cut-throats or for phantoms.

Human intuition is nearly always right, but human tuition is nearly always wrong, and in this book I will examine the meaning of these two forces, how instinct is true and how learning is so frequently false. It is the next war which vitally concerns us and not the last, and this next war I believe will be very different from the last, and here is my first repetition. Quite possibly, when Europe is once again aflame, those already enlisted may find the army a safer habitation than an office in Lombard Street. Then, in place of witnessing the Israelites fleeing to Brighton, shall we behold them flocking to Great Scotland Yard!

J. F. C. F.

Café des Aveugles,
November 20, 1922.

CONTENTS

The Reformation of War

PROLOGUE

COMMON-SENSE

PHILOSOPHY is a love of wisdom, and wisdom is the power of forming the fittest judgments from whatever premises are under consideration. Philosophy is, therefore, an evolutionary system of thought which has as its objective the survival of the fittest thoughts. While animals progress through the struggles of body, humankind, as distinct from animals, progresses through the struggles of mind, but with this difference: that, while in animal life every unit must struggle in order to survive, in human life the struggles of one great brain will, on occasion, remould an epoch. We find, therefore, that human beings may be divided into two categories—the masters (supermen) and the slaves (super-monkeys); in fact, into creators and imitators. This has always been so, and is likely to remain so, for without the second there can be no opposition to the first, and opposition is the manure of progress, and progress, seemingly, is of the will of God.

If the aim of wisdom is to arrive at the fittest judgments, then, indeed, is common-sense the true philosophy of life. To do the most appropriate thing at any moment is what is generally known as a common-sense act; in other words, common-sense may be defined as: " thought and action adapted to circumstances."

Common-sense is the secret of the masters, but to the slaves it is the greatest of all heresies, for to doubt that "thought and action are adapted to conventions" is to them the one unforgivable sin. In the great masters common-sense is not only spontaneous but prescient, for not only are actions adapted to circumstances, but the circumstances themselves are seen in advance of their happening. In this form common-sense is known as "genius," which, in nature, is creative and not formative; that is to say it produces wholes and does not merely set together parts. Genius may be classed, therefore, as masculine in character, for it produces the seed of a new life, while labour, the work of the slaves, is feminine, for it takes many months, many years, to build the finished article, and, then, it frequently spoils it in the process.

In the philosophy of common-sense there is no absolute truth, and, whether the absolute exists or not, it does not fall within its purview; metaphysics have but a very subordinate place in the realms of common-sense, the normal sphere of which is the existing and the evolution of the actual.

The absolute, especially under the conception of the absolute truth, is the undying cause of mental warfare. Millions of brains have thought upon this subject, hundreds of thousands of books have been written to explain it, and, worst of all, millions of lives have been sacrificed in the wrangles, quarrels and disputes which have arisen through its questing. To the multitude, this search after the incomprehensible has worked like some deadly drug. To them it has invoked false dawns to still-born days. To them, for a moment, it has shattered darkness, it has tantalized them with unreachable things—fraternity and the death of strife; it has shown them the squalor and sordidness of their surroundings, and then it has left them, dazzled and squinting, with the meanness of their thoughts, the smallness of their hearts, and the impotence of their souls, to scramble back into the night which knows no dawn, breathing profane words and groping after moonbeams and shadows.

The absolute may be "The Pearl of Great Price" . . . The Stone of the Wise" . . . or "The Lamp of Illimitable

Light." For the great it may be the " Universal Solvent," but for the multitude, and the world is made up of multitudes, it is with the rush-light of common-sense that we must seek to guide humankind, lest they be utterly blinded. For them, progress is not to be sought for in the solution of some infinite equation, but in the banishing of phantoms and the pricking of many-coloured bubbles; for each man carries about with him a book of lies—his preconceived thoughts, and lives in a world shackled by Euclidian lines—his fears and prejudices. Each word must be rewritten, each line dissolved, and he who can replace " length without breadth " by a cobweb, frees humanity until the web be broken. Slavery is the self-damnation of the credulous, and it must ever be remembered that most men are mental malingerers.

In the philosophy of common-sense, the goal is contentment, and, to the multitude, this goal is symbolized by health and happiness. Hitherto, so I feel, the great peace and war thinkers have given to the crowd speculations and uncertainties, vociferations and the ululation of words, full of meaning to themselves, possibly, but unintelligible to their servants : sterile words, words which cannot sprout or wax, inert words without blood or sap, cold words without warmth or fire. Words which, being either not understood or misinterpreted, cause wrangles, arguments and quarrelling—truly unbalanced things and, therefore, contrary to common-sense which aims at an equilibrium of reason and action.

To the masses of humankind there are three happinesses in this world—sex, food and freedom. " Kiss, eat and do as we like." Thus, towards the abbey of Theleme do they wend their way, bickering about things spiritual and material, their very longings being filled with the itch of war. They pluck dead fruit and in anger they turn on one another, one saying : " What profiteth a man if he gain the whole world and yet lose his soul," and another with blasphemy replying : " A pair of boots is more important than all your Madonnas."* Thus

* " Memoirs of a Revolutionary," Krapotkin, vol. ii. 86.

are the masses rent, one side seeking some infinite desire, and the other some finite balsam. Thus, between the absolutism of both is the grist and chaff of life ground into war. Proportion is lost ; there is no give or take ; life grows rigid, laughter ceases, one side cries " vice " and the other " virtue." The veil of the temple of peace is rent, and behind it grins the god of war—that panic mystery of progress.

Common-sense merely shifts these points of view, bringing them within one focus. Vice is the salt which gives life its savour —true ! Like a patch on a girl's cheek, it accentuates a beauty which is not its own. Vice, in fact, is the spur which sets virtue in motion.* The savour of life is its virtue, and yet this savour is far from being the mere salt, which, of itself, leads to unquenchable desire. The common-sense man does not inveigh against vice or exalt virtue ; when contentment does not exist, and discontent is war, he harmonizes these two. He does not seek a universal balsam, but a human anointment by an integration and agreement ; not an absolute truth, but an equation of circumstances which will be true—that is, will be righteous as long as these circumstances exist. He seeks the best at any given moment and not the best for ever. He is the arbitrator, and, like a good judge, he is so rare a being that, once he has harmonized one set of differences, he should not be allowed to take root ; he has his circuit and should journey from one discontent to another, so that his energies may never slacken and ever find new worlds to conquer.

In war common-sense plays a similar part. If peace be called virtuous and war vicious, then it is in the harmonization of their differences and not in the permanent state of either that a solution to righteousness must be sought. To understand this righteousness we must understand what peace and war entail.

* " Vice, crime, disease, decay and death are just as natural and necessary events as virtue, health, growth and life ; ever present processes that are kept in check while evolution is in full vigour, they will increase when it has reached and passed its height : their presence and functions now are the augury of a larger presence and function some day."—" The Pathology of Mind," Henry Maudsley, p. 192.

We must understand man as man, and the contentedness and discontentedness of man as human and not as metaphysical problems. To-day we stand at the parting of the ways, behind us lingers an old-world conception rooted in the events symbolized by " 1815." In front of us is cast the shadow of a new era which, in its time, will be symbolized by " 1918." Both were conceived in peace, both were born in war. Nations must either move or perish, they dare not wait for miracles to reincarnate them, for to wait is to paralyse the will to act. This will is the true wand of the magician, that sceptre of common-sense which rules the orb of human reason.

Thoughtful reader, common-sense has been my rush-light, it has lit my path through the chaos of past wars and, by the glimmer of its flickering flame, I have attempted to peer down the rugged track of future warfare, that track which at some uncertain day to come will once again loom into a great highway of strife along which will tramp those legions yet unborn. How wends the trail, what of the country it traverses ? Is it mountainous or rocky, wooded or a region of swamps ? And what of those yet distant warriors, are they armed as to-day, are they of the past or for the future ? Have they common-sense emblazoned on their standards, or do they advance under the faded banners of tradition ? Are their actions adapted to the circumstances which will then confront them ? Do they aspire after miracles, or drunken are they on the valour of ignorance, or are they equipped with that unshakable confidence begotten of imagination and nurtured by foresight ? These, in all modesty, for learning has made me doubtful, are some of the questions I shall attempt to answer. The book now opens : fare thee well !

I

THE ORIGINS OF WAR

THE philosophy of war and the philosophy of life are but synonyms for that system of knowledge which resolves human phenomena into their causes by an analysis of the struggle for existence. This struggle, though science differentiates between organic and inorganic, eventually finds its source in the molecular and atomic energies of matter and in the energy of the ether itself. Beyond these, human understanding, at present, is unable to penetrate.

We start with the known, the world as we think it to be, as it has seemed to us and is likely to continue to seem; we travel into the unknown, yet ever before us and behind us hang the curtains of the unknowable, distant in places, close touching here and there. Through these we cannot see, even with the eyes of uttermost imagination. Though war and the struggle for existence may cease, could we but penetrate this veil, all our inferences so far go to prove that, on this side of it, war is an ultimate factor in Nature as she reveals herself to us through the limitations of the human mind.

We think we can, symbolically, picture to ourselves a state of complete inertia, just as we think we can picture to ourselves the shape of a fourth dimensional figure, but, in reality, such a state is incomprehensible, though in some form or another it is innate in every human heart. The religiously minded seek the life eternal, where there is no marriage or giving in marriage; in other words, no duality; likewise the city clerk he also seeks, even if an inadequate, yet a fixed wage so that he may be relieved from the horror of plus and minus quantities. Thus, throughout life itself, do we see on the one side a desire for rest, and on the other a desire for activity in order that rest may some day be accomplished.

I will postulate that we do start with inertia, the unknowable ; then, let us picture to ourselves, how we cannot say, that an activity is begotten within it : this activity then is war, whatever may be its complexion, for it will produce within inertia, a vibration, a disruption, a tearing and rending asunder. Henceforth, we have a duality—tendencies towards rest and tendencies towards activity, stability and mobility, a clash between these two in the ether, in matter and in life. Thus has the roar of war deafened the uttermost limits of eternity before the stars twinkled or the sun shone, and, as far as the human mind can fathom, is likely to resound through these abysmal depths until the universal blankness of inaction covers the infinite with its pall of perfect peace.

This desire for peace, and for the peace which passeth understanding, is innate in the heart of man : " anything for a quiet life," is the cry of the millions which surround us. It forms their spiritual goal, which is quite unattainable since Eve ate of the apple—henceforth " in the sweat of thy face shalt thou eat bread, till thou return unto the ground." Allegory though this may be, Eden is not of this life, for, though the lion may be brought to lie down with the lamb, the struggle for existence will still continue. Lambs will go on nibbling the young grass, and lions will die of indigestion, and the world will be peopled with gambolling foolish folk who, eventually, will find their normal level through the horrors of over-production. Thus does Nature instil the battle in one form or another in order, presumably, to improve the stock, so that the curse of Eden may be accomplished.

Though the desire of man is peace, the law of life is war ; the fittest, mentally or bodily, survive, and the less fit supply them with food, labour and service. Life lives on life ; look around and see if this be not true, and though the majority of human kind has given up cannibalism, many are still meat eaters ;

nevertheless, quite possibly the flesh of animals may also, some day, become revolting to the palate, and men may even gasp with horror at the idea of boiling a turnip. The advent of synthetic food will, however, in no way alter the law of life, though it may change the convolutions of the intestines ; for operate this law must, in the pulsations of the amœba and in the vibrations of the highest mind of that super-race with whom, for nearly three thousand years, we have been persistently threatened by revolutionaries—yet we remain human, ever and always human, and this is the keystone in the arch of our philosophy.

Thus it will be seen that the pendulum of life swings between two extremes—fear and love, and though man desires rest, the hand which holds the balance has ordained that he must seek it through activity. Man possesses no right to live, but solely might to kill and so to preserve life ; this is his one great birthright which holds good not only for primitive man but for human society as it is organized to-day ; for do not we find that, in most countries, in order to curb this might, the penalty is death, that is the very exercise of it, or imprisonment for life, which is but a delayed execution at the public expense ?

True, man desires life, for it is sweet to live ; he desires life, and though there can be no right in this desire, it is the strongest of his instincts, the instinct of self-preservation—the ultimate source of all human sorrow and of all human joy. This instinct urges him to protect his life, to preserve it, to link his life with that of woman, to duplicate their lives in the lives of their children and to protect this duplication. In the family, primæval or of to-day, there is a human right—protection, which in its turn, like an arch, rests on the abutments of physical strength and mental cunning. The stronger survive through brute strength, and the more cunning through craft ; thus begins that interminable struggle between muscle and mind which is the mainspring of all progress.

In the primitive family man is the hunter, he has but one object in life—to kill ; to kill for food, to kill for warmth and to kill for protection ; his impulse is purely an active one. With woman it is otherwise, her desires are not active but restful. In place of killing, her will is to preserve life. She prepares the food supplied to her by her husband, the hunter ; she suckles her children, she fashions the home. Habit teaches her order, from order emerge customs and laws. In her long lonely vigils, while her man is on his bloody quest, she dreams, and from her dreams are born the gods, and from the contemplation of her children, as they roll in the grass at her feet, is conceived the stupendous vision of immortality.

In the family is born the spirit of co-operation, that working together for the common good through an integration of ideas and by a division of labour. Then families struggle with families, conquer and coalesce, and tribes emerge and are welded into nations. And, when history opens her gloomy portals, there stands War—the god of creative destruction, that grim synthetic iconoclast.

I will now examine this struggle, not from the point of view of the so-called " Realities of War," so frequently described by shell-shocked war correspondents, but from that pivotal point— the human instincts.

All human activities are ultimately girt by a mysticism unfathomable to the reason, which may only be sensed by a vague irrational intuition. The mentality of the great captain is difficult to analyse ; frequently, he is a student, but study alone will not create him ; frequently, he is inordinately brave, but neither will courage alone differentiate him from the herd. Possibly he is but the focal-point of his epoch, fashioned by the very circumstances which he eventually controls by fusing with them his own creative power. Identifying his power with that of his age, he concentrates it and wields the new creation like a weapon ; conjuring forth the primal instincts always latent in man, he leashes and unleashes them, and men follow his touch, harnessed as they are to his will and he to theirs. This awakening of the primitive instincts is one of the most mysterious forces in war, a force which, if understood, will show that either wars are inevitable, or that the excitement which goes to engender them must, during peace time, find a healthy outlet if they are to be kept in leash.

The dormant instincts in man, once let loose, normally crystallize round a leader, who, in the eyes of his followers, becomes a super-man, a power to be venerated. During life his creative mind controls them, but, when dead, his spirit petrifies, and what was once the focal-point of individual energy becomes the static tombstone of collective idolatry. An image is raised; though called by his name it is soulless, it breathes no new word, neither can it move, for it is lifeless, it is but a make-belief.

Round this image congregate the priests of the cult of war; their words are his words, but his words are dead words, words of the past, which now bear little relationship to truth, who never stays her onward step. Doctrines grow into idolatrous dogmas, so that the worship of idols replaces the belief in living things. It is thus that nations are destroyed through the crystallization of ideas in traditions and stagnation of effort due to lethargy of thought.

From the military aspect, such idolatry as this does not only mean unprogressiveness in the science and art of war, but also aggressiveness towards indulging in war, this aggressiveness being due to two main causes:

(i.) The valour of ignorance of the nation.

(ii.) The barbaric stimulus of the army.

The first is due to a lack of power to control policy. Nations are always competitors, especially great civilized nations, and, consequently, the weaker is forced to accept the will of the stronger, and, when the weaker happens to be a prosperous and wealthy nation, this acceptance of the will of the stronger, and sometimes less prosperous, is irritating. So much so is this the case that the weaker, not being able to adjust by force the balance to its favour, resorts to craft. Craft leads to secrecy, and secrecy to suspicion and discontent, which frequently lead to an open quarrel between the parties concerned, the one not knowing the intention of the other.

If we now examine modern history, we shall find that, though military might has sometimes detonated wars, the most prevalent detonator has been diplomacy ; craftiness and especially diplomacy which attempts to make good a deficiency of power by an excess of duplicity, for this type of craftiness ends in contempt. Diplomacy in its turn is spurred on by national ambitions which, in a wealthy nation, are many and complex. These, even though unsupported by power, breed among the ignorant masses a valour based on the ignorance of the requirements of war and, frequently, force diplomacy to offer veiled or open threats, though the diplomatists themselves fully realize that this process can only succeed through bluff, and if their opponent pays to see the hand, seeing it he will laugh and most certainly take the pool. A nation, even more so than an individual, is sensitive to ridicule, for the masses possess little wit, and it is ridicule, in its various simple and complex forms, which is a sure irritant of war.

As the first is due to a lack in the equilibration of power between two or more nations, so is the second due to the existence of a hiatus between the mentalities of the nation and its army. National progress seldom can be stayed even by the will of the majority, because, on account of competition, an evolution of the old hunting spirit, the minority, by compulsion the thinking (more crafty) section of the community, can seldom be brought to concentrate wilfully on its own destruction. Its tendency, anyhow, is to live and not to die. It frequently arises, however, especially in prosperous nations, that the national will to hunt for wealth is so great that it monopolizes all their efforts, and, consequently, that little thought is given to the maintenance and protection of their wealth through military action. In these circumstances, an army, which should be *of* the nation, becomes separated from it. It develops into a caste, and, being neither looked upon with affection nor cared for, it loses pace in the race of national progress and becomes barbaric by growing out of date. Then, when diplomacy fails, and the national equilibrium is upset by insult or ridicule, the nation, which is ever a heterogeneous crowd swayed by its primitive instincts, receives its impulse from its army and its military leaders ; this impulse being mainly subconscious. Reacting by suggestion on the crowd mind, it detonates war even before the nation is prepared to accept it, and the result is, frequently, a disaster.

A barbaric army, that is, one separated in intellect from the nation to which it belongs, is an incentive to war without being an efficient weapon wherewith to wage it. Civilization cannot safely progress under the protection of such a force ; consequently, all that goes to build up the mentality of a nation must go to build up the mentality of its army. These two must be one in mind, one in soul and one in body, though this does not necessarily mean that the whole nation must consist of drilled soldiers, but that the soldiers and civilians, in thought and progress, are living in one camp.

The pathology of war may be traced to a decay in or retardation of the mystic impulses which, springing from the instinct of self-preservation, control the destinies of nations. The true might of a nation is to be sought for not so much in the strength or perfection of its army, which is but the means of materializing this might, but in the health of its spirit, that is its will to preserve itself from dangers internal and external. This spirit or vitality, so necessary to its existence, finds its outlet through the two primitive instincts of hunting and breeding. Hunting evolves into the pursuit of commerce, which, when stabilized in a civilized State, becomes labour without excitement. The natural pleasures of life are denied, cramped and crushed, day in and day out, by a monotonous routine. The stimulus of the hunt being absent, the body becomes lethargic and the mind dulled by a grim monotony. When such a state eclipses the soul of a nation, the primitive instincts gather in stormy clouds. Then man's mind broods and is filled with the gloom of discontent ; he becomes nomadic in spirit, the old desire of the forests and the jungle is awakened in his soul, it flames forth like some subtle lightning, and there is war. The pent-up instincts have flashed forth, man is once again the healthy heathen, the roamer over the mountains and the reveller in the mists. The intoxication of the chase is upon him, the instincts of millions of years are unleashed. He is freed for a space from the fear of death. Now for the nation is there glory in death, in self-sacrifice and renunciation, as there was once glory for man in risking his life in the winning of his mate and in the protection of his family and his lair.

To reduce life to a geometric figure, with its Euclidian laws, its parallels which never meet and its mathematical lines and points, is not only to suppose that life is an inert substance, but that humanity is governed by reason, which it most certainly is not. For, if it be the exception rather than the rule for any two rational individuals to agree on any one argument, how much more so is not this the case when opinions are being discussed collectively ? Reason is indeed a potent faculty of the mind, but it is only one of a number of potent faculties, all of which ultimately are swayed by the primitive instincts. Further, it is the first to volatilize directly the stimulus of fear is applied to the sympathetic minds of a crowd of persons.

The more geometric the life of a nation becomes, the more are its instincts and desires pent up, and the more do they attempt to find some outlet for their vigour. During the Middle Ages the greater part of Europe was shrouded under a religious pall, and the horror of the static state rested on the Western World like a huge coffin lid. Had not crime and cruelty given an outlet to man's natural appetites, the world would have gone mad ; as it was, it was half insane ; and only war and brutality prevented it becoming totally so. To-day, we possess religious freedom, yet democracy, the new cult, is fast foisting on to us a static organization. The State is replacing the Church, and State domination must end in geometricity of thought and action, the enslavement of the individual and the charging of the Leyden cells of war. There can be nothing more appalling to the philosopher than to watch the doctrines of those with universal brotherhood on their lips, percolating through society like water through a rock, when it is apparent, by universal inference, that these doctrines will one day solidify and break the nations saturated with them into a thousand fragments.

To restrict the ravages of the worst of all wars, namely, civil war, which is a crime against Nature, since in place of preserving national existence it destroys it, there is implanted in the heart of man an impulse which directs the energies of all progressive nations externally against those which surround them. This impulse is the first cause of organized wars ; it is the instinct of self-preservation seeking security by establishing unattackable frontiers. In primitive times a tribe could only feel secure when the tribes surrounding it were less powerful than itself ; if equally powerful, then warfare was incessant until the strongest gained inter-tribal supremacy. To-day it is much the same, strong nations cannot tolerate strong nations as neighbours, and are only deterred from attacking them if the balance of international power is against them. Their impulse of self-preservation bids them extend their frontiers to impassable or easily defensible obstacles, or else to nations so inferior in military strength to their own, that they have nothing to fear. In the case of England, in spite of her secure frontiers—the sea, this impulse is constantly active. Her history is free from serious revolutions, because the hunting spirit of her people expended itself in adventure, such as that which led Drake around the globe. Cromwell, though the child of revolution, in his wisdom so completely directed this spirit externally that no revolution of a serious character has since his day occurred in England. For self-preservation, England's frontiers are the sea coasts of other nations, and, when land frontiers are impossible to avoid, she has nearly always attempted to protect them by the creation or maintenance of weak buffer States.

The second great cause of war is in nature economic. In primitive times, pillage, or the killing of one man by another for personal gain was a common act. As civilization advances, this personal act is replaced by a tribal or racial act of war. A tribe is killed off and its belongings taken, and, if its land be annexed or occupied, in nature, such a war becomes organized, since permanent garrisons are created. Thus far the natural history of the primitive form of war, evolving into the organized, is simple. Not so, however, its evolution through the psychological channels. To steal a man's meat undoubtedly calls, in a primitive people, for vengeance ; so also does any detraction from a man's prowess, for it lowers him in the eyes of his family and so attacks him psychologically by wounding his vanity. To degrade a neighbouring tribe to serfdom or slavery is to attack it psychologically on wholesale lines. If the tribe be effete, it will probably die out ; if virile, it will probably rebel and attempt to purge itself of its masters and so regain its former freedom. The same applies to the enslavement of nations, and in order to obviate such a catastrophe, nations raise armies to protect them against so oppressive a fate.

As a war of vengeance generally originates from a war of pillage, so does a war of purgation normally arise from an act of conquest, and conquest, in its modern sense, may be viewed under three economic headings.

(i.) The conquest of land in order to obtain raw material.
(ii.) The conquest of man-power in order to manufacture commodities.
(iii.) The conquest of free markets in order to sell commodities.

All three of these types of conquest may be accomplished without the clash of steel, just as the enslavement of a weak tribe by a strong may be accomplished by fear or by a moral threat. But, if the original owners of the land, the man-power enslaved, or the possessors of the markets, are virile, bloodless though these conquests may be, they frequently lead to the most bloody of wars of purgation, because conquest generally carries with it a restriction of the primitive hunting instinct in the conquered.

From the national standpoint, a war of conquest has nothing whatever to do with right or wrong, for Nature knows nothing of morality, unless morality be defined as race survival. Efficient races conquer and enjoy their conquests, just as efficient hunters kill and enjoy their prey. So also are effete races conquered, and, should they be eaten up, they deserve their fate. If they can, however, overthrow their conquerers then equally do they deserve their liberation. A race which submits to slavery is a race the virility of which has grown sterile. Nature abhors a mental eunuch as fervently as she abhors a physical vacuum.

Great nations are born in war, because war is the focal-point of national concentration ; great nations decay in peace, because peace is the circumference of the circle the centre of which is this focal-point—the greater the diameter or time the greater the danger resulting.

From the material aspect of war, chiefly through the sexual instinct, is evolved a nebulous and later on a fixed psychological character. Man has to win his mate by being the strongest of his sex ; should his strength fail him, he must resort to craft, which is synonymous to insulting the strength or abilities of his opponent by taking what might to-day be called a mean advantage of him. He lurks in the bushes or in the shadows of night and assassinates, rather than fights his competitor. Such a type of attack, from the physiological standpoint of the survival of the fittest, is revolting to the strong, and it must be remembered that it is the physiological aspect of war which is always the most prominent in man's mind. Such an act as this is " unsportsmanlike," it is comparable to shooting a fox in a hunting county, or attacking a lion with a machine-gun in a game preserve. It cries for vengeance, for, if it succeed, there will be scant protection for the offspring of even the strongest. From the wars of muscle against muscle is thus evolved the war of brain against brain, in the form of personal vengeance. The antagonist is not killed for his belongings, but in order to get rid of him as an individual and later on as a public nuisance. Vengeance grows into morality, which may be defined as : that state of existence which best enables the individuals composing society to live peacefully together. Morality is not an instinct but a compromise ; from it evolves legislation, which metes out punishment to those who injure peaceful race survival. As politics are dependent on the will of the majority, a will which is never for long stable, to endeavour to establish an international code of laws on a footing similar to that of national legal codes is to attempt the impossible, for without political power the legislation of politically irresponsible courts is valueless ; for political power is based on the will of the majority of a nation, which, in its turn, is governed by the instinct of national preservation.

The evolution of wars of vengeance is exceedingly intricate. First, they are pursued to avenge personal injury, the theft of another man's belongings—his flint arrow-heads or his wife. Secondly, to avenge the theft of his sentiments—slander against his person or the deprivation of the affection of some woman. As such, wars of vengeance are as common to-day as 50,000 years ago. Thirdly, they develop into protecting the race from insult and depredation, and, when races depend for their existence upon commerce, they direct their efforts against dishonest and underhand practices. Fourthly, they develop into avenging insults directed against the political and religious systems of nations, and here we find vengeance based on a multitude of capricious ideas. The Arian schism hinged on the word " Homoousios," and a war between England and Spain, in 1739, on the severance of an ear. These pretexts cannot be considered as real causes of war, but rather as the detonators of the pent-up hunting instinct in man which has been tamped down by artifice. Society may be likened to a permanent powder magazine formed of innumerable sentiments. When these are scattered and far spaced, the danger of explosion is small, but when concentrated one spark may lift the roof off a generation.

In all these phases of war, whether slow and internal or rapid and external, whether directed against individuals or nations, whether military or commercial, the sum total of horror is purely relative to the state of the sentiments of the day—they are dynamite or crude black powder ! Thus a war, to-day, between the Americans and Japanese, waged in order to obtain human flesh for food, would freeze the blood in the heart of every

2

European outside Russia, even if it resulted in only a few dozen
people being eaten. After prolonged periods of absence from a
certain condition, its occurrence becomes a novelty, a new
creation which appals the inert mind. Such minds can find no
comparison wherewith to measure the cataclysm, though, if these
minds were by nature introspective, they would realize that, as
science has ameliorated the conditions of peace, so equally can
science ameliorate the manners of war.

In war, novelties of an atavistic nature are generally horrible ;
nevertheless, in the public mind, their novelty is their crime ;
consequently, when novelties of a progressive character are introduced on the battlefield, the public mind immediately anathematizes them, not necessarily because they are horrible but because they are new. Nothing insults a human being more than
an idea his brains are incapable of creating. Such ideas detract
from his dignity for they belittle his understanding. In April,
1915, a few hundred British and French soldiers were gassed to
death ; gas being a novelty, Europe was transfixed with horror.
In the winter of 1918-1919, the influenza scourge accounted for
over 10,000,000 deaths, more than the total casualties in killed
throughout the whole of the Great War ; yet the world scarcely
twitched an eyelid, though a few people went so far as to sniff
eucalyptus.

One of the main arguments against armies is their futility ;
but, if this be true, this argument can with equal force be
directed against peaceful organizations ; for surely it is just as
futile to keep vast numbers of a nation on the brink of starvation
and prostitution, as happens in nearly all civilized countries
to-day, as it is to keep an insignificant minority of this same nation
on the brink of war.

Human nature, fortunately, is not changed by wild illogical
statements or even by logical comparisons. Petronius Arbiter,
eighteen hundred years ago, wrote in his Satyricon :

" As for Trimalchio, he has as much land as a kite can fly over,
he has heaps upon heaps of money. There is more silver lying in
his porter's lodge than another man's whole estate is worth. And,

as for slaves, wheugh! by Hercules, I do not believe one tenth of
them know their own master."

Substitute factory hands for slaves, and the Rome of Nero is
not very different from the England of Tennyson :

" Peace sitting under her olive, and slurring the days gone by,
   When the poor are hovell'd and hustled together each sex, like swine :
   When only the ledger lives, and when only not all men lie ;
   Peace in her vineyard—yes ! but a company forges the wine."

This, say you, has all been changed, democracy has to-day
unhovelled the multitudes, and Socialism is offering to the world
a new and beautiful future. This future is, however, nothing
more than a mirage of the past—material gain and greed, eagerly
grasped at by the hungry. I will quote again :

' Why do we prate of the blessings of Peace ? We have made them a
     curse ;
   Pick pockets, each hand lusting for all that is not its own ;
   And lust of gain, in the spirit of Cain, is it better or worse
   Than the heart of the citizen hissing in war on his own hearthstone ?
   But these are the days of advance, the works of the men of mind,
   When who but a fool would have faith in a tradesman's ware or his
     word ?
   Is it peace or war ? Civil war, as I think, and that of a kind
   The viler, as underhand, not openly bearing the sword."

In spite of the shrieking peace-mongers, the fact is that the
state of peace is the state of war, and the horror of peace is the
horror of war ; this may not be rational, but it is, nevertheless,
true, true even if history be only but an indifferent witness. It
is here that we merge into the purgative character of wars of
vengeance—fevers begotten by communistic social rule, which
restricts the outlet of man's natural appetites. Wars of revolution are caused by despotism, the worst form of which is communism, not only the communism of the gutter but the communism of bureaucratic government. All men are proclaimed
or treated as equal, the law of the survival of the fittest is ab-
rogated in a mist of words and in a flow of ink ; the struggle for
existence is abolished, and the immediate result is that it asserts
itself in its most brutal forms. Sentiments group themselves and

concentrate, and the magazine of society becomes sensitive to combustion at the slightest moral shock.

Philosophically, there can be no end to war as long as there is life or motion, for the very elements struggle in ceaseless combinations and, as far as we can at present judge, will continue to struggle until the crack of doom. The greatest world-war which our globe ever experienced was a bloodless one ; it occurred millions of centuries ago, when the earth, then an incandescent cloud of gas, tore itself away from the sun its mother and with flaming caul proclaimed its identity. From this great war all others have originated and will continue to evolve progressively, ever tending towards some unknown goal.

Modern wars are, in the main, progressive in nature, for they sweep aside obsolete laws and customs which have lost their meaning and spur men awake to the realities of life, so that they may cease for awhile dreaming of life's little troubles. To prohibit wars of conquest, if such a prohibition were possible, and to permit wars of purgation would end in a universal catastrophe. If rigidly adhered to, such a policy would lead to complete isolation of each separate nation, to an end of commerce and an end to the exchange of ideas. Such a state is inconceivable, and human wars, it is thought, as the Buddhists proclaim of sorrow, can only cease with a cessation of desire.

Henry Maudsley, the eminent psychologist, accentuates this very clearly in this book " The Pathology of Mind," when he writes :

> " Have not nations owed their formation as much to brotherly hate as to brotherly love—more perhaps to the welding consolidation enforced by the pressure of hostile peoples than to the attractive forces of their components ? And what is the spur of commerce but competition ? War in one shape or another, open or disguised, has plainly been the divinely appointed instrument of human progress, carnage the immoral-seeming means by which the slow incarnation of morality in mankind has been effected.
>
> When we look at facts sincerely as they are, not satisfied to rest in a void of speculative idealism and insincerity, we perceive that in every department of life the superior person uses his superior powers to the inevitable detriment of the inferior person, even

though he may afterwards dispense benevolently out of his super-
fluity to some of those who fall by the wayside. The moral law
only works successfully as a mean between two extremes, excess
of either being alike fatal. He who aspires to love his neighbour
as himself must at the same time take care to love himself as his
neighbour, making himself his neighbour while he makes his neighbour himself; his right duty being to cultivate not a suicidal self-
sacrifice which would be a crime against self, but just that self-
sacrifice which is the wisest self-interest and just that self-interest
which is the wisest self-sacrifice. So he obtains the utmost development of self within the limits of the good of the whole. He will
not go very far in morality if he compound for lack of self-renuncia-
tion on his part by a special indulgence of his own self-love in
dictating sacrifices to other people. Were men to carry the moral
law of self-sacrifice into rigorous and extreme effect they would
perish by the practice of their virtues. When they had succeeded
in eradicating competition, in making an equal distribution of
wealth, in prolonging the feeblest life to its utmost tether, in banishing strife and war from the earth, in bringing all people on it to so
sheep-like a placidity of nature that they would no more hurt and
destroy, and to such an ant-like uniformity of industrious well-
doing that no one would work for himself but every one for all,
they would have robbed human nature of its springs of enterprise
and reduced it to a stagnant state of decadence. A millennium
of blessed bees or industrious ants ! For it is the progress of desire
and the struggle to attain which keeps the current of human life
moving and wholesome alike in individuals, in societies, and in
nations. Not to go forward is to go back, and not to move at all
is death."

If progress be rendered impossible, only two other courses
are open to humanity : stagnation or retrogression. The first
means war, as we know it to-day, and the second, war as it was
known in the past. Retrogression can only lead to one goal,
the goal we started from, a sliding back into the brute, in which
process of retirement we shall have to pass through all past
phases of human warfare until, naked and unarmed, we tear
each other to pieces with our nails.

To weep and gnash our teeth over preparations for war,
because they cost so much, is but a symptom of decadence.
" How can we afford these ships or these armies ? " This is
the whine of a small householder and not the cry of a virile
nation. Neolithic man wept similar tears, no doubt, over his

arrow-heads. " How can I afford all these days chipping this wretched flint, my body aches for food and my brood is starving ? " He did afford those days, and had he not done so, his race would have been exterminated. Nature cares nothing for the sweat of man's brow or the leanness of his purse ; nations must, therefore, not only afford to survive but must *will* to do so. If some war commodity be beyond the national means or the national powers of labour, nations must not cease in their efforts or rely on second-rate weapons, but, instead, they must either increase their powers of labour or substitute for these costly weapons cheaper and more effective ones. The nations which can accomplish this survive ; those which can-not—perish. Nature tolerates no unearned rest : " In the sweat of thy face shall thou eat bread," this is her irrevocable dictum. There is no permanent rest for humanity. Forwards lie the pains of growth, backwards the agony of decomposition. To stand still is to rot. The Saurians are dead and gone, yet the little ant survives and multiplies.

As to the functions of the State, the State should remain inert, that is to say it should so govern a nation that equal opportunity for the evolution of all creative and receptive brains is rendered possible. This is not communism, which aims at assisting the weak, but race survival, which aims at assist-ing the strongest to forge ahead through the agency of a virile competition. It has little to do with the distribution of wealth, but everything to do with the catholicism of health. Some will continue to be born rich and some poor ; nevertheless, it should be a national point of honour that no stone be left unturned which will enable all to be born strong, and to be provided with equal opportunities of education, of marriage and of law. The function of the State is to level the social tilting ground for the national tourney between thought and action ; to see that for either side it is free from pitfalls, and that there is no hitting below the belt. As long as the State does not produce this condition of impartial inertia, so long will wars of purgation arise and lead to wars of conquest. When all States do produce it, as unsentimentally as a judge administers justice, then indeed may collective acts of brigandage become as infrequent as their individual counterparts. Bellona will not have ceased to be, but she will have changed her complexion from a tawny red to a leprous grey. Battlefields will become bloodless, and the agony of muscle will be replaced by the agony of mind. To drive a nation mad may then quite possibly be considered a superb victory. Thus does civilization stride forward on the stepping stones of death and madness towards life and the fullness of life, until her path is lost in the gloom of an inscrutable future.

Be this as it may, " the will to live " is the ultimate horizon of her philosophy. Far distant may this circumference grow in ever increasing circles, but, in the centre of these, squats their originator, a shadowy form, all but indiscernible to the philosopher, totally unseen by those filled with windy words : the form of primitive man, gorged on the flesh of his prey and basking in the sun.

II

THE SCIENCE AND ART OF WAR

HAVING now analysed the soul of war and, rightly or wrongly, having assumed that wars in one form or another are inevitable, in this Chapter I will examine the science and art of the mind and body of this subject. I do so because, when we come to consider the future tendencies of war, not only is it important to realize that future warfare must be an evolution of present and past warfare, but that all forms of warfare are founded on a common science.

From a cursory study of military history, a student might well be deluded into believing that war is so closely related to the roulette table as to be classed as a veritable game of chance. What does he see ? The efforts of many noted generals who have been either gamblers pure and simple, or else keen but inept dabblers in dark sciences. These, he soon finds, have worked much like the alchemists of the Middle Ages, who sought for perpetual motion, the universal solvent, the philosopher's stone and the elixir of life, in mixtures compounded of dragon's blood, grated unicorn's horn and the marrow of consecrated cats.

Even in the Great War of 1914-1918 we can discover few scientific reasons for the innumerable actions fought, no firmer basis than Marshal Saxe could discover in his day when he wrote :

> " War is a science so obscure and imperfect that, in general, no rules of conduct can be given in it which are reducible to absolute certainties ; custom and prejudice, confirmed by ignorance, are its sole foundations and support."

The armies of 1914 were imitators of past methods of warfare, for they had been fed on past battles. Science does not imitate, for science unravels and creates.

What is science ? Science is co-ordinated knowledge, facts arranged according to their values, or to put it more briefly still and to quote Thomas Huxley, science is " organized common sense . . . the rarest of all the senses."

War is as much a science as all other human activities, and, like all other sciences, it is built upon facts, of which there are an innumerable quantity. From these facts may we extract the elements of war and the principles of war and the conditions of war—the circumstances in which the principles must be brought to govern the elements.

What is the simplest possible type of human warfare ? A fight between two unarmed men. What is their object ? To impose their wills upon each other. How do they accomplish this ? By giving blows without receiving them or the fewest possible number. In these words have we completely laid bare the essential nature of the fight, in fact we have discovered the pivotal problem in the science of war—the destruction of the enemy's strength (physical or moral), which not only embraces his army but the whole of his nation, and which constitutes the crucial problem in the art of war: " how to kill, disable, or capture without being killed, disabled, or captured."*

In war we start with man, the author of all human strife. To defeat his adversary he must will to do so, he must move towards him, he must hit him and he must prevent himself from being hit, or, otherwise, he may fail to impose his will, which is enforced and protected by his actions.

Man, in himself, may be compared to the ether, out of which the other elements are evolved. In war the physical elements arising out of the body of man are : movement, weapons and protection.

* This is the traditional problem. Later on I will show that for body should be substituted mind.

Examining movement first, we find that, tactically, there are two types: protective movements and offensive movements; the first I will denote by the term " approaches " and the second by that of " attacks." In the former the one thought of the soldier is " to prevent himself from being hit," and, in the latter, " to hit his enemy." The more he can hit the less he will be hit, consequently, indirectly though it may be, not only is the whole action protective in character, but it becomes more and more so as the offensive succeeds. From this it will be at once seen that any idea of thinking of the offensive and the defensive phases of war, battle or duel, as things in themselves apart, is absurd; for these two acts form the halves of the diameter of the tactical circle, the circumference of which is the fight. They are, in fact, the positive and negative poles of the tactical magnet called battle.

Of weapons there are two types—hitting and hurling weapons. The first I will call " shock weapons," such as the bayonet, lance and sword, and the second " missile weapons," such as arrows, bullets, and gas. As the tactical object of physical battle is to destroy the enemy, which is best accomplished by clinching with him, the infantryman's offensive weapon is the bayonet and his bullet is his defensive weapon, on account of its ability to protect the advance of the bayonet. Thus, we see that, whenever two weapons of unequal range of action are employed, the one of longer range is always the defensive weapon and the one of shorter range the offensive one, and even if three or more weapons be used, this holds equally good for all. From this appreciation may be deduced a tactical rule of the highest importance: In all circumstances missile weapons must be employed to facilitate or ward off the shock.

Protection, or the defensive, has little to do with holding positions or beating back attacks, for it is just as much part and parcel of every forward movement as of every holding or retrograde one. I have already pointed out how the bullet defends the bayonet and how the approach secures the attack by lessening casualties when the soldier is advancing and not actually using his weapons. Both these forms of protection are indirect, that is to say, they do not ward off blows but impede blows from being delivered. Besides these indirect means of protection, which include the use of camouflage and smoke clouds, several direct means have frequently been employed, such as armour, earthworks and fortifications. Under this heading, to-day, must also be placed the anti-gas respirator. Direct protection is such as will nullify the effect of blows. Mobile direct protection is generally the most effective, for any change in location necessitates a change in the enemy's tactical organization, and consequently a loss of time for destructive effect. When, as in a tank or battleship, mobile direct and indirect protection can be combined, the highest form of security is obtained; this fact was all but unrealized in the last great war, though a study of the art of war in the Middle Ages will show that it formed the tactical backbone of the combat between armoured knights.

I have already made mention of the fact that to imitate is not necessarily to work scientifically. Science extracts knowledge from the unknown by applying to it certain laws which universal inference has established. Thus we have the laws of gravitation, of causation and of evolution. War has also its laws or principles, and they are to be found in the duel as in the battle. As regards these principles of war there has been much discussion of an unscientific nature. Before the Great War of 1914-1918, every Field Service Regulations made mention of principles of war and pointed out their importance, but did not name them. The British Field Service Regulations of 1914 stated: " The fundamental principles of war are neither very numerous nor in themselves very abstruse," and then left the readers in complete doubt as to what they were. Some twenty years ago Marshal, then Lieut.-Colonel, Foch wrote a learned book on " The Principles of War," in which he mentioned four, and then, apparently in doubt as regards the remainder, placed " etc." at the end of this list.

There are eight principles of war, and they constitute the

laws of every scientifically fought boxing match as of every battle. These principles are :

>   1st Principle.—The principle of the objective.
>   2nd Principle.—The principle of the offensive.
>   3rd Principle.—The principle of security.
>   4th Principle.—The principle of concentration.
>   5th Principle.—The principle of economy of force.
>   6th Principle.—The principle of movement.
>   7th Principle.—The principle of surprise.
>   8th Principle.—The principle of co-operation.

No one of the above eight principles is of greater value than the other. No plan of action can be considered perfect unless all are in harmony, and none can be considered in harmony unless weighed against the conditions which govern their application. Seldom can a perfect plan be arrived at because the fog of war seldom, if ever, completely rises. It is, however, an undoubted fact that the general who places his trust in the principles of war, and who trusts in them the more strongly the fog of war thickens, almost inevitably beats the general who does not.

These principles are, in my opinion, of such importance, being in fact the governors of war, that, as far as space will permit, I will consider them in detail. First, then, what is the objective in war ?

(i.) *The Principle of the Objective*. The object of a nation is national preservation, which, in a civilized race, may be defined as honourable, profitable and secure existence. Here we find three sub-objectives, an ethical objective, an economic objective and a military objective. These three combined I will call the political objective or policy of the nation, the stability of which depends on the will of the people.

In modern warfare it does not pay to outrage the sentiments of the day, neither does it pay to destroy the economic resources of the enemy. Consequently, when all peaceful methods of settlement have broken down and a nation is reduced to military action in order to maintain or enforce its policy, its object should be to impose its will with the least possible ethical and economic loss not only to itself but to its enemies and to the world at large. A nation which wins a war through foul play degrades itself in the eyes of other nations and loses the trust of the world. A nation which destroys the economic resources of its enemy, destroys its eventual markets, and thus wounds itself.* War must entail some loss, but the less this loss is the greater will be the victory; consequently, the military object of a nation is not to kill and destroy, but to enforce the policy of its government with the least possible loss of honour, life and property. If the enemy can be compelled to accept the hostile policy without battle, so much the better. If he opposes it by military force, then it should never be forgotten that the strength of this force rests on the will of the government which employs it, and that, in its turn, this will rests on the will of the nation which this government represents. If the will of the nation cannot directly be attacked, then must the will of the army protecting it be broken. In the past this will has been attacked by attacking the flesh of soldiers, and, so consistent has this been, that the idea has arisen that the military object of war is to kill and to destroy. Thus, in the popular and military imaginations, the means have obscured the end; consequently, the prevailing idea of all parties in the recent war was destruction, to destroy each other, and so blinded were they by the means that they could not see that in the very act they were destroying themselves, not only during the war but in the peace which must some day follow the war.

I believe that the world is slowly learning this lesson, and that, as in my opinion wars are inevitable, the old idea of warfare based on destruction will be replaced by a new military ideal, the imposition of will at the least possible general loss. If this be

---

* It is true that a self-supporting nation does not suffer in proportion to one not self-contained, but it must be realized that ecomomics and ethics are closely related, and, even if destruction does not economically affect the destroyer, the ethical repercussion resulting through the bankruptcy of the victim is very likely to wound him morally.

so, then the means of warfare must be changed, for the present means are means of killing, means of blood; they must be replaced by terrifying means, means of mind. The present implements of war must be scrapped and these bloody tools must be replaced by weapons the moral effect of which is so terrific that a nation attacked by them will lose its mental balance and will compel its government to accept the hostile policy without further demur. In this book I will show the probable nature of the first stage in this new evolution of war; meanwhile, I will examine war from the present military aspect.

In organized warfare, if the objective cannot be gained by political action, recourse is made to force, the military objective being the defeat of the enemy's military strength so that his national policy may be transmuted. This objective is attained by a harmonious employment of the remaining seven principles of war. Without a definite objective there can be no definite military policy or plan, and without a policy or plan, actions cannot be co-ordinated; consequently, the principle of the objective may also be considered as the principle of co-ordination, for, as Napoleon once said : " There are many good generals in Europe, but they see too many things at once. I see the enemy's masses and I destroy them." By this appreciation of the objective all his movements were controlled.

According to the objective depends the direction taken by an army, and on its direction depends its supply. The enemy is at A, we are at B. Does the line joining these two points give us our direction ? Yes and no ! Yes, if the seven remaining principles are not adversely affected by our moving in this direction, and if the conditions permit of us doing so. No, if otherwise. We should not, however, discard this direction off-hand, even if we find that some of the principles are difficult to apply ; instead we should test each possible line of advance until we arrive at the line of least resistance, bearing in mind that the principle of the objective aims at creating such a situation as will force the enemy to accept the policy he is fighting against.

(ii.) *The Principle of the Offensive.*   Will the objective that we have selected enable us to apply the principle of the offensive ? If it will not, then the objective selected must be discarded, for the offensive in war is the surest road to success.   If it will, then in which direction should the offensive be made ?   The answer to this question depends on the conditions of war (existing and probable circumstances), which should be looked upon as the correctors of all military movements.

Thus, if time be against us, time in which an enemy can mass his reserves to meet our offensive and so outwit us, the offensive becomes futile or dangerous ; unless, possessing more men than brains, our object is simply to kill as many of the enemy as we can, regardless of cost, which is not only a violation of the principle of economy of force, but the poorest of poor generalship. A private soldier thinks in terms of killing men, but a general should think in terms of disorganizing and demoralizing, that is of defeating armies.   " Push of pikes " is a simple game compared to defeating an army, which requires an acuter intellect than that of a lusty halberdier.

Seldom will it be possible to march straight towards the enemy's main force in order to defeat it.   Its whereabouts may be unknown, but, even so, the ultimate objective—disorganization and demoralization, remains constant.   Consequently, though many acts may be required before the curtain of victory is finally rung down, each act must be a distinct progression towards the transformation scene of peace.   If this be not the case, then an infringement of the principle of the objective will take place.   This must be guarded against, for each blow must form a definite link in an offensive chain of blows, in which moves, as in chess, are seen ahead.

A general will seldom win without attacking, and he will seldom attack correctly unless he has chosen his objective with reference to the principles of war, and unless his attack is based on these principles.   Imagination is a great detective, but imagination which is not based on the sound foundation of reason is at best but a capricious leader.   Even genius itself, unless it be stiffened by powerful weapons, a high moral, discipline and training, can only be likened to a marksman armed with a blunderbuss—ability wasted through insufficiency of means. Conversely, an efficient army led by an antiquated soldier may be compared to a machine gun in the hands of an arbalister.

(iii.) *The Principle of Security*. The objective in battle being to destroy or paralyse the enemy's fighting strength, consequently the side which can best secure itself against the action of its antagonist will stand the best chance of winning, for by saving its men and weapons, its organization and moral, it will augment its offensive power. Security is, therefore, a shield and not a lethal weapon, consequently the defensive is not the strongest form of war, but merely a prelude to the accomplishment of the objective—the defeat of the enemy by means of the offensive invigorated by defensive measures. The offensive being essential to success, it stands to reason that security without reference to the offensive is no security at all, but merely delayed suicide.

As danger and the fear of danger are the chief moral obstacles of the battlefield, it follows that the imbuing of troops with a sense of security is one of the chief duties of a commander, for, if weapons be of equal power, battles are won by a superiority of nerve rather than by a superiority of numbers. This sense of security, though it may be supplemented by artifice, is chiefly based on the feeling of moral ascendance due to fighting efficiency and confidence in command. Given the skilled soldier, the moral ascendancy resulting from his efficiency will rapidly evaporate unless it be skilfully directed and employed. Ultimately, as in all undertakings, civil or military, we come back to the impulse of the moment, that is to the brains which control each individual nerve which runs through the military body. To give skilled troops to an unskilled leader is tantamount to throwing snow on hot bricks. Skill in command is, therefore, the foundation of security, for a clumsy craftsman will soon take the edge off his tools.

The basis of strategical security is the soundness of the

general plan of action, the infrequency of the change of objective or of direction, and of the absence of unnecessary movement. Strategical security is also arrived at by placing an army in a good position to hit at the communications and headquarters of the enemy while protecting its own : by so disposing a force that it may live at ease and fight efficiently.

Grand tactical security may be defined as the choosing of a vulnerable target or the refusal to offer one. Here the factors are mainly those of time and space—the rapid massing of weapons at the decisive point whether for attack or defence, and the general organization of the battle itself. Minor tactical security embraces the entire gamut of a soldier's actions : his individual moral and efficiency, the quickness and audacity of his leader, the judgment and determination of his commander and the confidence of his comrades, as well as the superiority of his weapons, means of movement and protection.

(iv.) *The Principle of Concentration.* Concentration, or the bringing of things or ideas to a point of union, presupposes movement ; movement of ideas, especially in an army, is a far more difficult operation than the movement of men. Nevertheless, unless ideas, strategical, tactical and administrative, be concentrated, cohesion of effort will not result ; and in proportion as unity of action is lacking, so will an army's strength, moral and physical, be squandered in detail until a period be arrived at in which the smallest result will be obtained from every effort. The central idea of an army is known as its " doctrine," which, to be sound, must be based on the principles of war, and which, to be effective, must be elastic enough to admit of mutation in accordance with change of circumstances. In its ultimate relationship to human understanding, this central idea or doctrine is nothing else than common-sense, namely, action adapted to circumstances. The danger of a doctrine *per se* is that it is apt to ossify into a dogma and to be seized upon by mental emasculates who lack the power of analytic criticism and synthetic thought, and who are only too grateful to rest assured that their actions, however inept, find justification in a book

3

which, if they think at all, is, in their opinion, written in order to exonerate them from doing so. In the past, many armies have been destroyed by internal discord, and some have been destroyed by the weapons of their antagonists, but the majority have perished through adhering to dogmas springing from their past successes, that is self-destruction, or suicide, through inertia of mind.

Though an army should operate according to the idea which, through concentration, has become part of its nature, the brain of its commander must in no way be hampered by preconceived or fixed opinions, for, while it is right that the soldier should consider himself invincible, it is never right that the commander should consider himself undefeatable. Contempt for an enemy, however badly led, has frequently led to disaster ; therefore it is the first duty of the commander to concentrate on common-sense, and to maintain his doctrine in solution so that it may easily take the mould of whatever circumstances it may have to be cast in. Strategy should be based on this doctrine of action adapted to circumstances, and, consequently, concentration in strategy may be defined as making the most of opportunity and also of forecasting and foreseeing the possibility of opportunity before it arises.

As strategical actions chiefly depend on means of movement, so equally does the concentration of the forces engaged in them depend on communications ; consequently, from the network formed by the lines of supply is evolved grand tactical concentration, the object of which is to overcome resistance by breaking it down or turning it to advantage.

From the point of view of the battle itself, concentration has for centuries been based on the maxim of " superiority of numbers at the decisive point," because numbers were the coefficient of weapons, each man normally being a one-weapon mounting. This maxim no longer holds good as a general rule, and in its place must be substituted : " superiority of moral, weapons, means of movement and protection." Men, in themselves, are an encumbrance on the battlefield, and the fewer men we employ,

without detracting from sufficiency of weapon-power, the greater
will be our concentration of strength, for the aim of concentration
is as much concerned with securing an army against blows as it is
with enabling an army to deliver them.

(v.) *The Principle of Economy of Force.* Economy of force
may be defined as the efficient use of all means : physical, moral
and material, towards winning a war. Of all the principles of
war it is the most difficult to apply, because of its close inter-
dependence on the ever changing conditions of war. In order to
economize the moral energy of his men, a commander must not
only be in spirit one of them, but must ever have his fingers on the
pulse of the fighters. What they feel he must feel, and what they
think he must think ; but while they feel fear, experience dis-
comfort and think in terms of easy victory or disaster, though he
must understand what all these mean to the men themselves, he
must in no way be obsessed by them. To him economy of force
first means planning a battle which his men *can* fight, and secondly,
adjusting this plan according to the psychological changes which
the enemy's resistance is producing on their endurance without
forgoing his objective. This does not only entail his possessing
judgment, but also foresight and imagination. His plan must
never crystallize, for the energy of the battle front is always
fluid. He must realize that a fog, or shower of rain, a cold night
or unexpected resistance may force him to adjust his plan, and,
in order to enable him to do so, the grand tactical economy of
force rests with his reserves, which form the staying power of the
battle and the fuel of all tactical movement.

On the battlefield, to economize his own strength and by
means of feints and surprisals to force the enemy to dissipate his,
is the first step towards victory. Every weapon which he can
compel the enemy to withdraw from the point of attack is an
obstacle removed from the eventual path of progress. Every
subsidiary operation should be based on the objective and effect
a concentration of weapon-power on the day of decisive action.
Every subsidiary action should add, therefore, an increasing value
to victory, that is the power of producing a remunerative tactical

dividend. " Is the game worth the candle ? " This is the question every commander must ask himself before playing at war.

By this I do not mean that risks must never be taken, far from it, for it is by taking risks which are worth taking that, more often than not, the greatest economies are effected and the highest interest secured. In war, audacity is nearly always right and gambling is nearly always wrong, and the worst form of gambling in war is gambling with small stakes ; for by this process an army is eventually bled white.

Economy of force is also closely related to economy of movement. Many generals have attempted to win a military Marathon in sprinting time. They have thrown in all their reserves at once, and so have lost their wind within a few hours of the battle opening. Such operations as these are doomed to failure long before the first shot is ever fired.

(vi.) *The Principle of Movement.* If concentration of weapon-power be compared to a projectile and economy of force to its line of fire, then movement may be looked upon as the propellant and as a propellant is not always in a state of explosive energy, so neither is movement. Movement is the power of endowing mass with momentum ; it depends, therefore, largely on security, which, when coupled with offensive power, results in liberty of action. Movement, consequently, may be potential as well as dynamic, and, if an army be compared to a machine the power of which is supplied to it by a series of accumulators, should the object of its commander be to maintain movement, he can only accomplish this by refilling one set of accumulators while the other is in process of being exhausted. The shorter the time available to do this the more difficult will the commander's task be ; consequently, one of his most important duties, throughout war, is to increase the motive power of his troops, which depends on two main factors—moral and physical endurance.

In war, the power to move must first be considered in the form of the general will to move. In battle the forward impulse comes from the leaders and the troops themselves. They are, in fact, self-propelled projectiles and are not impelled forward by the explosive energy of command. Such energy scarcely if ever exists; what does exist is direction to its impulse, and the reinforcing or recharging of this impulse with more power by means of reserves. These reserves not only endow the combatants with physical energy but with a moral sense of power and security which impels them forward.

Even with an army of high moral, that is to say an army which possesses the will to move towards danger, or, inversely, the will to refuse to move away from danger, it must ultimately be the physical factor, the muscular endurance of the men themselves, which sets a limit to their power of movement. In order to increase muscular movement, by conserving it as long as possible, mechanical means of movement have for some time been employed for the strategical and administrative movements of an army; so much so that the approach movements to-day are based on locomotives and lorries. The result of this is that, while strategical mobility, namely movement at a distance from the enemy, has enormously increased, tactical movement, through increase of impedimenta, has decreased in inverse proportion, until battles founded on muscular movement have become more often than not static engagements based on broadside fire from fixed positions. In order to overcome this immobility, mechanical cross-country movement has been forced on armies, and, whatever may be the prejudice shown to its introduction, the complete replacement of muscular movement by it is as near a certainty as can be foreseen.

(vii.) *The Principle of Surprise.* Lack of security, or a false interpretation of the principle of security, leads directly to being surprised. The principle of surprise, like a double-edged tool, is an exceedingly dangerous one in unskilled hands; for, being mainly controlled by psychological factors, its nature is less stable and the conditions affecting it are more difficult to gauge.

Surprise, in its direct meaning, presupposes the unexpected, which, throughout history, may be considered under five general headings :

   (i.) Surprise effected by superiority of courage.

   (ii.) Surprise effected by superiority of movement.

   (iii.) Suprise effected by superiority of protection.

   (iv.) Surprise effected by superiority of weapons.

   (v.) Surprise effected by superiority of tactics.

To gain superiority in anything or any quality takes time, consequently we find that, although minor surprisals may be gained by seizing upon the right opportunities, the possibility of effecting major surprisals is based extensively on forecasts and preparations made during days of peace, especially as regards the nature and requirements of the next war, for the surest foundation of being surprised is to suppose that the next war will be like the last one. In modern times, similarity between wars has seldom occurred, as the most casual retrospect into military history will prove ; consequently, when a commander attempts to copy former battles, we find that an army is frequently surprised with its eyes open. It sees things coming, but, blinded by prejudice and shackled by tradition, it does not perceive their consequences, which are only realized when their causes have taken or are actually taking effect.

On the battlefield itself a general is frequently surprised by his own stupidity, his lack of being able to understand conditions or to apply to them the principles of war. His stupidity sometimes takes the acute form of completely misunderstanding the endurance of his men ; not realizing what they can do, he orders them to do something which they cannot do, and the result is chaos and loss of life. Surprise among troops, as among individuals, is largely a matter of nerves. The nerves of an army are not only to be found in the individual temperaments and collective suggestibility of the officers and men, but also in its staff organization. The trunk nerves of an army are its general staff, whose one great duty is to convey the impressions felt by the rank and file to the brains of their commander. If this be neglected the best laid plan will fail and paralysis of action will result in being surprised.

(viii.) *The Principle of Co-operation.* Co-operation is a cementing principle ; it is closely related to economy of force, and therefore to concentration, but it differs from both of these principles, for while mass is the concentrated strength of the organism and economy of force the dispersed strength which renders the former stable, co-operation may be likened to the muscular tension which knits all the parts into one whole. Without co-operation an army falls to pieces. In national wars, the value of co-operation is enormously enhanced, fusing, as it does, the body and soul of a nation into one intricate self-supporting organism. All must pull together, for such wars are the wars of entire nations, and, whatever may be the size of the armies operating, these should be looked upon as national weapons, and not as fractions of nations whose duty is to fight while the civil population turns thumbs up or thumbs down. Gladiatorial wars are dead and gone.

We find, therefore, that for us co-operation in war embraces the whole gamut of our Imperial existence, which means that during war one master mind must control the whole national machinery, in order to reduce the friction which its adjustment by many hands inevitably creates. Take, for instance, the government of a nation at war. If there be friction in the government, there is friction not only throughout the nation but throughout the army. No man can efficiently serve two masters, neither can two masters lead and direct the same man. If in a cabinet of six members each strives to conduct a war departmentally, according to his own particular degree of ignorance in strategy, in place of one objective there will be six objectives, or, worse still, six phases of one objective. When such a state of affairs arises it is time to declare a dictatorship, for dispersion of force in war is to commit suicide while temporarily insane. There can be but one main objective ; consequently, all subsidiary ones must be reduced to their utmost limit to enable the concentration of all requisite battle-power at the decisive point. One objective requires one master-mind to formulate the general plan, and not half a dozen jacks of all trades to dissipate it. One master mind must control the war, and all other minds must accept or be compelled to accept his ruling.

Tactically, co-operation is based on battle organization, weapons, protection and movement, skill, confidence, discipline and determination : it is moral, physical and mechanical. This means that all must work for the attainment of the objective and not for themselves. The weeding out of fools and knaves is, therefore, the first step to be accomplished. The second is the scrapping of bureaucratic processes and shibboleths, and the bringing of ability to the top. Senility of thought is the antithesis of co-operative action. A vintage of new ideas is always produced in war, and the vats must be sufficient and the bottles strong enough to hold it ; for new ideas, like new wine, go through a process of fermentation, which in an army commanded by a weak-headed general can only lead to tactical intoxication. Co-operation in its widest sense spells not only military efficiency but national and Imperial efficiency, which centred round one line of direction impels all the life and fighting strength of the nation towards victory. Without such an axis an army fights floundering.

Principles in themselves are not worth the paper they are written on, for they are but mere words strung together in a certain order. Their value lies in their application, and this application depends on the thousand and one conditions which surround the elements of war during operations. What are these conditions, for without knowing them it is manifestly impossible to apply the principles ? Conditions are innumerable and ever changing, but the following are some of the most important : Time, space, ground, weather, numbers, training, communications, supply, armament, formations, obstacles and observation.

Each of these conditions may be considered as possessing a dual nature—a power of increasing the strength of the offensive and a power of increasing the strength of the defensive ; each, therefore, may be looked upon as possessing power to enhance offensive and defensive action in war.

A commander has three means at his disposal to deal with a condition :

(i.) He may avoid it.
(ii.) He may break it down.
(iii.) He may turn it to his own advantage.

The third course, which masters the difficulty, is manifestly the best, and it is the one which even a superficial study of military history will show was employed by the great Captains of war, it was in fact the secret of their success.

At the beginning of this Chapter I stated that, when two men fought their object was to impose their will upon each other. Up to the present I have mainly considered the means employed in order to accomplish this, and the principles governing these means. I will now turn to the psychological side of war, and show that it also has its elements, principles and conditions.

I will examine once again the primitive duel between two unarmed men, and from it will extract certain facts which may be classed as psychological elements. We first find the primordial material—man, but this time represented not by muscle but by mind. As the physiological object of the fighter is " to kill without being killed," so is his psychological object " to will without being willed." In these five words is presented the pivotal psychological problem in the science of war—the destruction of the enemy's will, which not only cements together his army but the whole of his nation in a vast living mosaic.

In war, as in all other phases of human activity, we find that the elemental psychological power is mind. In the case of our two unarmed fighters, both fear the other, there is no courage in the normal meaning of the word ; both desire to kill the other, and both instinctively take advantage of any opportunity to do so, especially, if by so doing, little risk be run. We here obtain three elements :

(i.) Will—desire to kill.

(ii.) Cunning—opportunity to kill at the smallest risk.

(iii.) Fear—desire to live.

The first is the mobile element, the second and third the offensive and the defensive elements respectively.

In primitive man, the first is awakened through threats to self- and family-preservation; in civilized man, though these bear equal sway, to them must be added the more recently acquired instincts of race- and national-preservation with all their ramifications—social, political and commercial. From the second, the making good of opportunity, we get a most complex evolution : cunning evolving into knowledge, education, science and art. From a tactical standpoint, natural cunning, as it presents itself in the primitive duel, evolves into the skill of the scientific fighter. Skill, reacting on the will, is a great incentive to moral, or confidence. The greater the skill of the soldier, the greater will this confidence become, and, as confidence in the weapons used plays as important a part in the growth of moral as skill in the use of the weapons themselves, we find that every improvement in weapons carries with it a psychological impulse. Thus, a man, who unarmed, will tremble before a footpad, feels no fear when covering him with a revolver. This is so important a point that it forms one of the main problems of this book. Weapons being material means of accomplishing mental impulses, not only do they stimulate the will by instilling confidence (moral), but skill in their use depends on this stimulation. Therefore, we find that, in order to control the third element, the mental powers of the soldier, as aggregated in his will, must never become slack, lazy or paralysed. They must be held in a state of attention on the " desire to win." This state of attention may be symbolized by the quality called " courage," which, in war, simply means a state of less fear than that in which the enemy is in, and not necessarily a sense of personal superiority such as might be felt by a poet or artist over a clodhopper or successful grocer. This state of courage, it will be seen, is equally dependent on skill in movement, weapons and protection, and the superiority of these elements themselves over those of the enemy. Thus, from will, through the reaction of cunning, which I will now call moral, and fear, is scientific fighting evolved.

Though the principles of war are equally applicable to the psychological aspects of this science, there are certain definite psychological principles which may be abstracted alike from the primitive duel and the scientific battle. There is, first of all, a desire or " determination " to fight, either on one side or both. The contest opens, therefore, with two wills in opposition. The giving and aiming of blows is made in order to enforce the will, and the avoiding of them to prevent the will being enforced. This enforcement I will call " demoralization," and the avoidance of it " endurance." From these we can extract three great principles :

(i.) The principle of determination.
(ii.) The principle of demoralization.
(iii.) The principle of endurance.

These psychological principles constitute a definite link between the physical and mental sides of the science of war, which may be depicted as follows :

MAN

$$\text{Muscle} \begin{cases} \text{Movement} . . \text{(Principle of Determination)} . . \text{Will} \\ \text{Weapons} . . \text{(Principle of Endurance)} . . . . \text{Moral} \\ \text{Protection} . . \text{(Principle of Demoralization)} . . \text{Fear} \end{cases} \text{Mind.}$$

We start with man physical and man mental ; he must possess the will to fight and the power to move, the connecting link is the principle of determination or the will to win. He must possess the moral to hit and the power to hit, here the connecting link is the principle of endurance. He must endow his adversary with a fear which will force him to protect himself or seek protection, which is acknowledgment of lack of endurance (temporary or permanent), and inferiority of determination ; here the connecting link is the principle of demoralization. Thus, we see that, in war, the " will to win " is the power of being able to endure and to demoralize, and that the three psychologica elements are not " things in themselves " but coefficients of the elements of war—movement, weapons and protection.

As I have dealt at some length with the principles of war, it is only fitting that I should now examine these psychological principles, for they are no less important. Briefly, the following are my views :

(i.) *The Principle of Determination*.   The limits of the principle of determination are first defined by the national objective of war, and secondly by its military objective. Between these two boundaries this principle operates.

From the national point of view, there is the will to impose upon the enemy's government a policy distasteful to it ; this policy must be clean cut, for on its stability rests the military objective, which psychologically is the " will to win." Subjectively, this will is concentrated in the mind of the commander, whose plan of action is the means of enforcing the national policy ; this plan must also be clean cut, that is to say it must be so simple that its very nature will give rise to the fewest possible complexities. As the stability of this plan will depend on the stability of the policy, the commander-in-chief must not only be acquainted with the nature of this policy, but with any changes rendered necessary through fluctuations in national conditions. Inversely, any changes in plan will entail modifications in policy ; consequently, we find that both the plan and the policy are correlatives, that is they are dependent on each other's stability. Now, as every policy must be plastic enough to admit of fluctuations in national conditions, so must each plan be plastic enough to receive the impressions of war, that is power to change its shape without changing or cracking its substance. This plasticity is determined psychologically by the condition of mentality in the two opposing forces. There is the determination between the two commanders-in-chief, and between them and their men, and, ultimately, between the two forces themselves. The " will to win " is, therefore, first of all a duel between two brains each controlling a weapon called an army ; and secondly, a struggle between two armies each equipped with various types of weapons. If all these various weapons, each influencing in its own degree the mentality of its wielder and that of his opponent, can be reduced in number, the principle of determination becomes more simple in application. If, again, similarity of protection becomes possible, simplicity is increased ; and if, finally, similarity of movement can be added, physically the simplest form of army is evolved.

I will now examine the psychological side. If the will and moral of each individual can be brought to a high but equal level and his fear to a low and equal level, the commander-in-chief will possess known qualities out of which to construct his plan. It will be seen, therefore, that, in its broadest sense, the principle of determination is the simplification of the means so that the will of both the chief and his men may become operative.

(ii.) *The Principle of Endurance.* Springing directly from the principle of determination is the great principle of endurance. The will of the commander-in-chief and the will of his men must endure, that is they must continue in the same state. It is the local conditions, mental and material, which continually weaken this state and in war often threaten to submerge it. To the commander endurance consists, therefore, in power of overcoming conditions—by foresight, judgment and skill. These qualities cannot be cultivated at a moment's notice, and the worst place to seek their cultivation is on the battlefield itself. The commander-in-chief must be, therefore, a mental athlete, his dumbbells, clubs and bars being the elements of war and his exercises the application of the principles of war to the conditions of innumerable problems.

Collectively, in an army, endurance is intimately connected with numbers, and, paradoxical as it may seem, the greater the size of an army the less is its psychological endurance. The reason for this is a simple one : one man has one mind ; two men have three minds—each his own and a crowd mind shared between them ; a million men have millions and millions and millions of minds. If a task which normally requires a million men can be carried out by one man, this one man possesses psychologically an all but infinitely higher endurance than any single man out of the million.   Man, I will again repeat, is an encumbrance on the battlefield, psychologically as well as physically; consequently, endurance should not be sought in numbers, for one Achilles is worth a hundred hoplites.

(iii.) *The Principle of Demoralization.* As the principle of endurance has, as its primary object, the security of the minds of men by shielding their moral against the shock of battle, inversely the principle of demoralization has as its object the destruction of this moral: first, in the moral attack against the spirit and nerves of the enemy's nation and government; secondly against this nation's policy; thirdly against the plan of its commander-in-chief, and fourthly against the moral of the soldiers commanded by him.   Hitherto the fourth, the least important of these objectives, has been considered by the traditionally-minded soldier as the sole psychological objective of this great principle.   In the last great war the result of this was, as I shall show presently, that the attack on the remaining three only slowly evolved during days of stress and because of a faulty appreciation of this principle during peace time.

I will now turn to the psychological conditions of war.

In considering these it must first be realized that all conditions are, in part at least, psychological.   That is to say they stimulate the brain in a greater or lesser degree; but while hundreds affect war materially, such as roads for supply and the influence of gravity on the flight of projectiles, thousands more directly affect the mind of the soldier, and through his mind his body, and through his body his actions.   Psychologically, we may divide these conditions into three general categories: those which are common to men either individually or collectively; those which affect the soldier as an individual, and those which affect a mass of soldiers as a homogeneous crowd.   The following are examples of these categories:

(i.) *General Conditions:* Safety, comfort, fatigue, catch-words, loyalty, honour, faith, hatred and cheerfulness.

(ii.) *Individual Conditions :* Knowledge, skill, determination, endurance, courage, imagination, confidence, talent and sense of duty.

(iii.) *Collective Conditions :* Suggestion, intuition, superstition, esprit de corps, tradition, moral, education, patriotism and comradeship.

I do not propose to analyse these conditions as it would take a long time to do so, nevertheless it should be remembered that the psychological principles in war cannot be applied correctly unless the conditions which go to build up soldiership have been stabilized, long prior to war, in days of peace.

The process whereby this stability is effected is called training. Training forms the true foundation of battle, which should be a continuation of the soldier's education, just as war itself should be a continuation of peace policy. For this to be possible it will be at once seen that training should not be based solely on the known conditions of past wars, but above all on the probable conditions of the next war. That, consequently, these conditions must be foreseen ; therefore, on the correctness of their forecasting will, to a great extent, depend the continuity of peace training in the form of battle tactics when war breaks out. Once we have diagnosed the conditions of the next war, then, by applying to them the psychological principles, we shall build up a scientific system of training. In fact, we shall start winning our battles from to-day onwards on the barrack square and in the class-room. Training, such as this, may well be called the art of war, the foundations of which I will now inquire into.

In analysing tactics, or the art of fighting, the military student usually visualizes the battle as a " thing in itself." The correct appreciation is diametrically opposite, for battles consist of a complex series of individual fights, each compounded of the elements of war operating concentrically round the problem of how to give blows without receiving them. This problem may be divided into four sub-problems, which every commander should consider prior to an operation taking place.

These four problems are :

(i.) How to keep men alive ?

(ii.) How to keep movement alive ?

(iii.) How to keep weapons alive ?

(iv.) How to keep moral alive ?

As the commander has four problems to solve so also has the soldier.   He has :

(i.) To hit his enemy while at a distance from him.

(ii.) To move towards him.

(iii.) To hit him at close quarters.

(iv.) To avoid being hit throughout this engagement.

The whole of these eight problems are in nature protective, and they form the foundations of offensive power, which endow it with stability of action as well as security during action and after defeat.

I cannot here do more than glance at this fundamental problem of battle organization : how to organize an army so that it possesses power of stability and mobility. Briefly it may be explained as follows : As the bones of man's body give stability to his muscular movement, so must every force of soldiers possess within their organization certain troops which can resist attack and certain others which can develop their mobility out of this resistance.   The battle of Crecy was virtually won by the English archers, the mobile element.   They could not, however, have accomplished what they did had not the men-at-arms and dismounted knights formed a stable base from which they were able to develop the full power of their bows.   A scientifically organized army is one which possesses a brain and a body, both of which possess a positive and a negative pole, stability and mobility. The stability of the brain is its faculty of reason based on knowledge, and its mobility the faculty of imagination based on the products of reason.   The military body is divided into two main forces : those which disorganize the enemy's brain and body—that is, break down its stability, and those which annihilate the broken fragments.   Each fraction of this body must possess power to resist movement and power to develop movement. Its mobility depends on a combination of weapons and movement, and its stability upon that of weapons and protection. From these two—its stability and mobility, are its offensive and protective powers reciprocally developed. Thus, in the hands of man, do we see a harmonious inter-relation between the three physical elements of war, and, according to the degree of harmony attained, do the plans of man succeed or fail. This brings us to the problem of grand tactics or battle planning.

In every plan the first question is to decide on the objective. In physical warfare the military objective is the defeat of the enemy's army, so that the will of his government may be attacked. Where, then, is the decisive point, the point at which the enemy may most economically be defeated ? The schoolmen answer: " The decisive point depends on circumstances," and some suggest a flank and others a central objective. The schoolmen, if they only thought in simpler terms than they are wont to do, could have long ago given a better answer to this question, which I will examine from a very simple point of view.

Every organization has one great prototype—the body of man. When a boxer fights another he tries to get a left or right on the side of his opponent's jaw. Why ? Not to break the jaw, the external body, but to derange the brain, the internal organ, because more than any other organ the brain controls the body.

The brain of an army is its command, and the command of an army is its decisive point, and no blow should be delivered without reference to this point. Though the brains of an army control its whole body, nevertheless the prevailing idea in tactics is one of brute force applied by weapons to the enemy's battle body. Batter the enemy's muscles blue and black and get battered black and blue in return, is the traditional method, and then only, when one side is rendered physically impotent, attack the brains !

I fully agree that more often than not it is impossible to strike straight to the jaw because our opponent carefully protects his chin. This does not, however, vitiate the fact that the decisive point is the command of the opposing army, and that the more

4

the enemy is forced to protect it, the less will he be able to hit out.

The elements of grand tactics are in essence very simple, once the decisive point has been agreed upon. The object is either to paralyse or disintegrate the enemy's command, which may be carried out by four acts, separate or combined. These four acts are:

(i.) *Surprise.* An enemy may be surprised, which implies that he is thrown off his balance. This is the best method of defeating him, for it is so economical, one man taking on to himself the strength of many. Surprise may be considered under two main headings: surprise effected by doing something that the enemy does not expect, and surprise effected by doing something that the enemy cannot counter. The first may be denoted as moral surprise, the second as material.

(ii.) *Envelopment.* An enemy may be enveloped and so placed at a severe disadvantage. Envelopment, whether accomplished by converging or overlapping, presupposes a flank, a flank which may be tactically rolled up, or, if turned, will expose the command and lines of communications behind it. The attack by envelopment is a very common action in war, which more often than not has led to victory.

(iii.) *Penetration.* An enemy's front may be penetrated in order directly to threaten his lines of communications behind it, or to hit at his command, or to create a flank or flanks to be enveloped. Normally, when once a hostile front is broken, the two sections are rolled up in opposite directions to each other, or one is held while the other is hammered; an operation which, if carried out successfully, usually leads to a total disintegration of the enemy's strength.

(iv.) *Attrition.* An enemy may be worn out by physical and moral action; this, though the usual method of defeating him, is also, frequently, the most uneconomical method, for the process of disintegration is mutually destructive.

Outside these four grand tactical acts of battle there is little to be learnt in grand tactics.

Once the direction of the decisive attack is fixed, the grand tactical plan is arrived at by applying the principles of war to the conditions under which war has to be waged ; in other words, liberty of movement has to be gained.   Free movement, which is the object of all strategy, is conditioned not only by impulse but by the form of the object moved.   In war, the will of the commander is the impulse, and the strategical distribution of his army the form of the military projectile, which should normally, like an arrow-head, be triangular, the main force in rear of it operating like the shaft behind the head.   Generally this head consists of an advanced guard and two wings.   The secret of all economical military formations is that they must possess a harmony of offensive and defensive power through movement, movement in its broadest sense being " locomobility," that is freedom of movement in all directions.

Liberty of movement is the basis of liberty of action, which is a compound formed out of superiority in the elements of war. It is the foundation of minor tactics and consists of the following values :

(i.) Man. .... { Superiority of will.
Superiority of endurance.
Continuity of co-operation.

(ii.) Movement.... { Superiority of speed.
Continuity of movement.
Superiority of manœuvre.

(iii.) Weapon. ..... { Superiority of weapons.
Superiority of clinching.
Superiority of fire.

(iv.) Protection .. { Inferiority of target.
Continuity of supply.
Superiority of mobile protection.

These must not only be mixed but amalgamated if liberty of action is to possess a practical value.   Thus, continuity of ammunition supply is useless if superiority of weapons does not exist ; and superiority of fire is useless if it does not

4*

produce continuity of co-operation. Liberty of action does not mean moving anywhere, but moving according to plan. It does not mean acting anyhow, either wholly or in part, but acting harmoniously towards the attainment of the objective. The relation of each of its components to the whole of its components, as represented by liberty of action itself, must be dynamic. Liberty of action is not the free will of the commander as a thing in itself, but the harmonious application of the principles of war to the conditions of the moment. The conditions formulating the lines of least resistance, and the will of the commander progressing, by means of the elements, along these lines according to the dictates of the principles. Liberty of action is the perfect correlationship between the elements and conditions by means of the principles. It is not so much the domination of one will over another as the adjustment of one will according to the other. Liberty of action is, therefore, the offspring of two wills rather than the force engendered by one ; it is the analogy of two opposites.

In an army, as a whole, liberty of action is expressed in the soul of the team. Each separate action is identified with the whole action of the army and not as a part of the whole ; it is a psychic power and not an organic act. It is manifested through a general will, a general endurance, and a general co-operation. It seeks action through a general mobility, a continuity of this mobility and the power of harmonizing it within itself. It attains result through the superiority of weapons, the superiority of fire, and the power of clinching, which it protects by the inferiority of the target offered to the enemy, the continuity of supply of ammunition, weapons, means of movement and men, and by the various forms of protection, the most important of which are of a mobile nature. Finally, liberty of action is based on harmony of movement, mental, physical and mechanical, which harmony, in itself, constitutes the energy of the compound.

If the nature of the elements of war is understood, and if we realize what is meant by liberty of action, it must, consequently, follow that there are both correct and incorrect offensive and defensive formations for weapons within units and for units themselves. I have already pointed out that the organization of every unit should possess stable and mobile qualities. I will now carry this analysis one step further.

In an attack, the first question to ask ourselves is: how to advance? The second: what will prevent an economical advance? Here again the old problem, of how to give blows without receiving them, confronts us. The clearance of obstacles to movement is essential; consequently, we arrive at a very common-sense answer, namely, that—few attacks except normal attacks are likely to succeed; in fact a normal attack should be what its name implies—an attack according to principles governed by conditions, i.e., economical.

Once resistance has been reduced to a normal condition; it logically follows that a normal formation can be devised which will suit this condition, and that, until this condition is arrived at, no formation will prove economical.

I have already explained that movement has two forms— the approach and the attack; consequently, there are two main formations in battle:

(i.) The approach formation: The fundamental formation for the approach is one which will combine mobility and security with potentiality of offensive power.

(ii.) The attack formation: The fundamental formation for the attack is one which will enable the maximum number of weapons to be used with fullest effect.

The normal approach formation is the column,* and the normal attack formation is the line.

Whether an offensive be carried out over open field land or against a strongly fortified position, its foundations are to be sought for in the base of operations from which the attack

* The smallest column is the infantry section in single file. It was used by Cyrus and Alexander; it was revived by Sir John Moore, forgotten, and once again to-day finds its place in infantry tactics. See " The Procedure of the Infantry Attack," by the writer, R.U.S.I. Journal, January, 1914.

is launched. In the past this base has been considered as the original starting line, and, if battles can be won in a single onslaught, this assumption is correct. As this can seldom be done, and as battles normally are won by relays of attacks, each relay must start from a stable base ; consequently there must be a base of operations to each objective requiring a fresh echelon of troops. Each echelon and each wave of each echelon must be sufficiently self-contained not only to be in a position to capture an objective, or line of resistance, but to hold it, and so form a base of operations for the echelon or wave following it. Further, each wave must be protected by the one in front of it as well as those behind it and on its flanks, and, as the first wave cannot be so protected and the last is frequently similarly situated, it is essential that the leading troops and those which will form the ultimate battle front should be drawn from a *corps d'élite*, the former setting the example and the latter instilling confidence.

Having now explained what I mean by a progressive base of operations, I will examine the action developed from this base. First, we have got to assemble the troops ; secondly, these troops have got to approach towards the enemy ; thirdly, they have got to attack him, and fourthly, destroy him physically or morally. Here we obtain four minor tactical acts :

(i.) The assembly.

(ii.) The approach.

(iii.) The attack.

(iv.) The pursuit.

The first is preparatory to the second, the second to the third and the third to the fourth.

The attack may be divided into two stages according to whether missile or shock weapons are used. These are :

(i.) The act of demoralization (fire fight).

(ii.) The act of decision (shock).

The act of annihilation or pursuit is virtually a new attack requiring fresh troops and troops of a more mobile nature to those pursued. To summarize :

A battle is an enormously complex action consisting of a number of simple parts. First, we must grasp the conditions, and, by so doing, ride the course. We then must take all the conditions which we know and weigh out their values in terms of assistance and resistance. Those we do not know but suspect we must consider even more carefully than those we know, allowing for a considerable margin of error, and always giving the benefit of doubt to the enemy.

Having collected and codified these conditions, we must next apply to them the principles of war. We must decide upon our objective, applying the offensive to those conditions which will assist us and security to those which will not ; thus shall we master conditions and harness them to our will. We then think in terms of concentration, of economy of force, of movement and surprise ; finally, we weave the whole together in a close co-operation.

By now our battle plan will have evolved almost unconsciously, and our plan is our grand tactics.

From this point we think purely in terms of fighting ; the skeleton is complete, all that now remains to be done is to clothe it with flesh and muscle—the elements of war. We think in terms of men, movement, weapons and protection. What are they all going to do ? Then human and animal endurance and communications, protection by armour, earth, fire and formation. All these give us our battle tactics. Then, there is the battle itself, in which the moral and physical powers of man come into play. The approach merges into the attack, and the offensive and defensive powers of weapons, shielded by direct and indirect protection, carry the man forward. Such is battle and such is war—a science and an art based on sure foundations, rooted fast in the past, with its boughs and leaves moving this way and that above and around us according to the conditions of the moment, but governed by the laws of existence—action and inertia.

III

THE ETHICS OF WAR

THE ethics of war is a subject which in the past has not been very carefully considered, and yet, without a just comprehension of it, it is quite impossible to sift the virtues of war from its vices. Hitherto, and from time immemorial, there have existed two opposite ethical schools of military thought—the peace-mongers and the war-mongers. To the first, war appears as the greatest of calamities and to the second, a beneficial necessity. Both, in the main, dislike war, but while the first seek its abolition through concord and disarmament, the second aim at its restriction through threat and preparation. In my own opinion there is right and wrong on both sides, for nothing in this world is absolutely good or absolutely evil, and the mere fact that in war an enormous energy is expended should lead every thinking man to suppose that, even if in the past this energy has been chiefly made use of for purposes of destruction, there may be some hidden path along which, should it be directed, prosperity in place of calamity will result. With this idea before me, it is my intention in this Chapter not so much to seek this path as to examine the values of war, for when once these are discovered the path itself should in the main become apparent.

Starting with an assumption that wars are an inevitable constituent of human progress, an assumption I have examined in Chapter I., I will first inquire into the ethical objective of nationality, for on this objective must the true military ethical aim be founded, because military might is but a means of enforcing national policy.

The science of ethics is the science of duty collective and individual. The duty of a nation is to survive ; first, with profit to itself, and secondly, with profit to humankind ; by which is meant that each succeeding generation should intellectually, morally and physically be superior to the generation which begat it. Ethics teach men their duties not only towards each other but towards themselves, and it is upon these duties that national stability is founded.

Race survival, or the struggle for existence between the weaker and the stronger, breeds cunning and co-operation, without which a nation must retrogress. Either the weaker in body must become more cunning (mentally able) in mind, or else they must unite co-operatively in order to survive. Consequently, weakness, as well as strength, possesses qualities of virtue and vice. Virtue, ethically, being defined as : those conditions which enable a race to survive, and vice as : those which accelerate its decline and hasten its extinction. Virtue and vice are, therefore, purely relative qualities, they are in no wise, in the Kantian sense, " categorical imperatives," but, in place, improvised factors conditioned according to local requirements. What is virtuous to-day may be vicious to-morrow, and what is vicious in the Antipodes may simultaneously be virtuous in the land of the Hyperborians.

Opposition, which presupposes weakness, is the incentive of mental progress both in the individual and in the race, for it constitutes the inhospitable region in which intellect *must strive* to live and either dominate or succumb. Mind fights muscle (superiority of human strength or numbers) with weapons of cunning which frequently turn conditions to the favour of the physically weak or outnumbered. Ethics have, therefore, little to do with moral customs established by majorities but much with the psychology of mind.

I have shown in Chapter I., how cunning threatens the existence of the strong—the cunning savage of primeval days lures his adversary away from security and kills him unawares. I also pointed out that this cunning, as a mean effort to survive, becomes repellant to the strong.   It is stamped as ignoble, for a scrofulous cripple may kill an athlete.   The idea of the human louse arises, an individual living on the mental deficiency of his neighbours, and the growth of this organism is restricted by laws and ethical codes.   Inversely, prowess is endowed with a nobility of character, for upon prowess is the physical health of the family or race founded, progeneration being a physical and not a mental act.

From prowess, especially the prowess of the male as he finds favour in the eyes of the female, is born the instinct of self-distinction, the personal ethical factor, which evolves into the collective ethical factor when it merges into race-distinction, and, eventually, into race-pride and patriotism.

If we inquire into the nature of these factors we shall find many components, some transient and some permanent.   Of the latter, the bulk may be placed under one common heading : the greatest ethical virtue or factor of either the individual or the nation being " common-sense."

The means of attaining the ethical objective of a nation is therefore common-sense. Honesty is common-sense ; truthfulness is common-sense ; courage is common-sense, because all these qualities assist in the survival of individuals and the race, and not only in survival but survival with profit through co-operation based on mutual confidence, trust and respect.

The reverse of common-sense is common-nonsense, a factor far too little appreciated. Thus a society in which every man lies is a nonsensical society ; so equally is one in which every man steals or every man cohabits with his neighbour's wife. Nonsensical periods, at times, sweep over a nation just as they do over an individual, especially during the periods of youth and decay (change). A spirit of comic opera, tragic enough to the actors but laughable to the onlookers, will sometimes possess an entire nation. They stamp out their intellect in a social delirium tremens, the product of imbibing strong doctrines to excess. They conscript their labour, socialise their women, and then, after an ebullition of liberty, equality and fraternity, whatever these intoxicants may mean, grab from each other whatever is left of their past prosperity and revert to honesty, truthfulness and moral conduct, because without these ethical factors it would be impossible for them to survive. They must either succumb to common-sense or perish nonsensically; this is the ethical law of survival.

If ethics be defined as " the science of duty," and duty, from its national aspect be defined as " the obligation to survive with profit," then ethics may be considered as the psychological aspect of biology, that is the science of life. Life never ceases to change, and, if ethics be a branch of this science, it, consequently, must be dynamic in nature, that is it must ceaselessly change coincidently with changes in man and in the society to which man belongs.

A moment's consideration will reveal to us that the motive powers in man are either instinctive or acquired, the former being far more stable than the latter; so also in ethics do we find a similar division. Psychologically, the instinctive qualities originate from the instinct of self-preservation and the acquired from innumerable artificial conceits springing mainly from that of self-distinction—the outer manifestation of the preservative qualities in the individual or race. The strong man advertises his strength brutally, he breaks the neck of a bull; the weak man's cunning slays the brute with a sharp flint or bullet. By openly demonstrating what each can do, they mutually teach the other their respective deficiencies and so exaggerate their intrinsic ability by swelling it with the admiration or envy of those who watch them, and, consequently, add moral power to their physical or mental strength.

In ethics, the process is very similar. We start with foundational or stable ethics, those based on the instinct of self-preservation; we progress through these codes to those of collective or social health, and through these to the codes of dynamic ethics, or the ethical comments arising through the mobility of changefulness in ratiocination and local circumstances. These, originating as unwritten rules of procedure, crystallize into customs and become petrified. Thence arise the internecine conflicts between instincts and acquirements—the social skeleton tries to shake off the withered flesh.

Thus, ethics may grow from a duty into a compulsion and evolve into a series of penal codes by which society is imprisoned and against which creative thought within society is ever striving, until, like a bodily fever, it sloughs the no longer sentient skin in a war of purgation. Ethics in the form of copy-book virtues are, therefore, a cause of war—wars of liberation which racially are endemic in character, that is contagious. One nation catching the psychological bacillus of liberty from another, is cast into a delirium in which the ossified ethical codes become mere " scraps of paper," social scabs, things to be torn up and scratched at by the instincts which are again freed from restriction. As restrictions no longer exist, they, like wild-fire, flow out athwart civilization and, on occasion, do not stay their fury until they have utterly consumed it.

Ethics, as customs, manners, conventional morals and fashions, are, when in a healthy state, mobile in nature. To discover whether any of these transient virtues are growing vicious simply requires the application of common-sense. That is, a comparison should be made between the effects of the doubtful virtue and the ethical objective—survival with moral profit, any deficiency being made good by action adapted to circumstances. Unfortunately, as common-sense is the rarest of all the senses, this simple process of gauging the temperature of the social body by this ethical thermometer is, more often than not, attempted by legal casuistry and a reshuffling of letters and words : an action which would do credit to an Assyrian sorcerer yelling barbarous names at the moon.

Besides those codes of morals which stimulate or restrict the evolution of the race, innumerable traditions exist both as stimulants and as narcotics. The power of tradition is immense, both as a beneficial influence and as a malevolent one, according to its relationship to circumstances.

Normally the origin of a tradition is to be sought for in

some successful individual action which has resulted in a betterment—intellectual, moral or material. Success depends, to a very great extent, on creative brain power and opportunity, which is nothing less than the exploitation of existing circumstances by existing means. This cause, as far as the individual is concerned, is temporary in nature. With a man's death his creative energy ceases, circumstances change and his theories of success lose their applicability.

In the individual, common-sense usually succeeds in pruning out dead personal traditions, because the individual nearly always possesses creative power of thought. The individual has to live on his own ability and energy, and, as an individual, he generally refuses to commit suicide by adhering to the obsolete traditions of his family ; besides this, these traditions, being for the most part unrecorded, die with their begetters. This is, however, far from being the case when traditions spring from collective acts or are absorbed by congeries of men. To the crowd the novel is, more frequently than not, the heterodox, because the crowd possesses little or no power of reason, and acts of individual ability irritate and insult it by diverging from what it accepts unthinkingly as established truths. These collective traditions grow into static and, frequently, meaningless shibboleths, which the receptively-minded accept without criticism, because they do not possess the ability to formulate it. They grow into vested interests and prejudices which clog all progress. He who has does not wish to part with what he has, even if it be but an irrational idea, and the more he is induced to part with it, the more prejudicial does he become. He fights the new idea, he slanders it, he anathematizes it, for progress is unpalatable to his static taste. He wishes to be left alone and do what his father and grandfather did before him, for what he has inherited, however rotten it may be, is a personal and treasured possession, it is part of himself, for acquisitiveness is an instinct in man.

When, in place of the individual, the crowd is considered, these vested interests and prejudices become deeply rooted in its nature, and in no assemblies is this more apparent than in those which represent religious orders, political denominations and military castes. Leaving the first out of account, I will examine the remaining two because they are closely related, every civilized army being managed by a political department of the government of the nation to which it belongs.

State departmental rule, I will assert before I prove it, is a system of management normally founded on common-nonsense, or upon action adapted to traditions in their static forms of interests and prejudices. What do we see?

A body of men precipitated into office from the test tubes of examinations which, at best, only prove the blotting-paper nature of their brains—their power of absorbing ink visually. Once deposited alembic-like on an office stool, the official process of mental distillation begins. A fixed salary sterilizes their creative powers; promotion by seniority demonstrates to them the uselessness of ability and the value of senility, and the prospects of a pension and the possibility of losing it, should they court disfavour, shackle and gag them—mind, nerve and jaw. They become monks in a monastic institution and repeat rituals which have lost their meaning, magical *mantras* which render their thoughts comatose to all reality beyond their files. They grow in strength and breed families called sub-departments; fill these with branch memoranda, which are revolved in never ceasing revolution like the prayer-wheels of the Mahayana Buddhists. It is so easy, so soothing, so absolutely safe—thus time, the controlling factor in life, is drowned in a sea of ink.

Then one day, these Trappists, fat on mental indolence, are awakened into the reality of a common-sense life outside them by seditions among those on whom they have successfully eked out their anæmic existence. War is in men's minds; creative thought is stalking through the land; the race instincts are once again abroad. But the monks cannot see them in their true form. In place they see devils, and horrified they return to their files, splash ink and rotate their wheels with as unchaste a frenzy as tame mice in a rotary cage. Thus are great nations periodically

inflicted with a fever by the insanitary mental conditions of
their government departments, their political incantations, their
prayer-wheels, their files, their ink and their lack of human-
touch.

In the armies of most modern States, we find the same cramping
influence of tradition at work and due to the same causes:
fixed pay, promotion by seniority and mental emasculation by
pensions. There is little or no incentive to creative thought
and every incentive to remain static. The whole atmosphere
is unethical, that is unprogressive; consequently, soldiers become
monastic in mind; they think in meaningless shibboleths, perform
unintelligible rituals, and base their duties on established rules
and the dotting of an " i " elaborately legislated for in some
obscure and rigid regulation. They are Homoiousians or Homo-
ousians in thought. The result of this is that it is not age which
renders them impotent to the realities of war, but the gelding-
knife of fixed ideas. Their thinking power is rendered sterile
by the darkness of unreality. Like weeds growing in a cellar,
so do armies become lank and lean in mind and colourless in
intellect by gazing at the walls of the mental dungeons in which
they are imprisoned.

Common-sense is again the remedy, common-sense which
replaces common-nonsense and which asks: " What is the
object of war ? " And which answers: " The security of
existence, prosperity and honour by the fullest exploitation of
the people and their resources." As long as this common-sense
question is not asked by the nation and the answer demanded
of its army, so long will this army remain an immoral association,
that is one which does not fulfil or guarantee the ethical needs
of the people. Salvation is through common-sense, which should
be the supreme canon and law of the military hierarchy.

During periods of stress, such as war, the character of a nation
reveals itself. If the war be unimportant, its loss may not
materially affect the nation, yet, nevertheless, it will be a blow
registered against its prestige, its moral capital upon the stability
of which so much of its material prosperity is founded. Its

credit will be lowered in the eyes of others, and a series of such blows may exhaust the national moral to such an extent that the prestige of the nation is laid bare to a knock-out blow. If the war be important, victory becomes vital, and the nation subconsciously realizing this, sets to work to divest itself of the formalities of everyday life. Traditions one by one are discarded and replaced by common-sense actions, and, as this process grows, the great stable and foundational race ethics reveal themselves, and the nation stands or falls on its character, to which is intimately related the justice of its cause.

Thus are the ethics of race progress frequently refined by war by being liberated from the jargon of meaningless shibboleths, the small-talk of politics and the strangling customs of bygone ages. War sweeps these aside like a storm of rain cleansing the foul streets of a dirty city. The process is uncomfortable, especially for those who are caught in the storm, but the result is the reinvigoration of the race through the self-revelation of its character. It finds that it possesses something more precious than conventions, grades, rules and regulations. It finds that, though these under certain conditions are inevitable, they are not essential, and to be purged from them, even but for a time, is a stimulus to the national health. It finds that it *has* a will to accept self-sacrifice and a soul above the pettiness of peace.

War is a great physician, a great medicine, a great purge. As the body of man, unless his body be exceptionally well regulated, requires an occasional aperient—a dose of calomel, so does a nation require an occasional war to free it from the costiveness of traditions; and, if foreign wars be rendered impossible, then Nature will simply replace them by internal revolutions. Thus we see that war may sometimes become an ethical factor of great value. This being so, I will now consider the nature of the ethical object of war.

As the military object of war is to defeat the enemy, and as the economic object is to add to the prosperity of the nation, so is the ethical object to enhance the national character, that is to increase its respect in the eyes not only of the enemy but of neutral nations. A man who fights cleanly is always applauded even if he lose; consequently, under certain circumstances, it is even more important to win the ethical objective than the military one; these circumstances depending almost entirely on the mentality of the combatants. If their ideals be of a material nature then the military objective becomes the most important; if of a moral, then the ethical objective is paramount.

In most cases the endurance of a war is based on the ethical nature of its cause. If race survival be this cause, then the war is founded on justice, and, as justice is a common-sense virtue, whether the artificial laws and customs of civilization prohibit wars or not, wars will continue, for the greatest of all laws is the unwritten and unwritable law of self and racial preservation. A man steals another man's wife: this is a definite common-sense injustice in a community where the men and women are numerically equal. Should, however, the number of women fall, I will suppose, to half that of the number of men, it is manifestly unjust to the race, whatever it may be to the individuals, that one man should have two wives or even that one man should possess one wife. Consequently wife-stealing ceases to be an act of injustice and becomes *of necessity* a natural virtue; for the strongest and most cunning will come into possession of the women, and, consequently, the race will prosper through an act which may be classed by the weaker party as one of the grossest injustice and immorality.

So also in war is the ethical process very similar; justice depending on the instincts which underlie civilization and the conditions which surround it, and not on the conventions which veneer it. If a war be waged for the personal benefit of individuals, it normally will prove a vicious war, but if for the benefit of the race, a virtuous one If, further, this war be fought not only for the benefit but for the self-preservation of the race fighting it, it will then become a common-sense war of necessity, that is a righteous war, which means, to refuse to wage it would be the grossest act of national immorality.

5

Great wars directed towards an ethical objective may consequently be looked upon as a new dispensation which breaks up the atheism of peace begotten by long periods of personal indulgence in place of racial improvement. Peace solidifies customs, and customs and traditions strangle the national will. Then comes war and sweeps these aside ; it ploughs through accepted dogmas and roots up the weeds of civilization, preparing the ground for the next and better crop. War proves a nation not only capable of mastering its enemies, but of mastering itself ; of sacrificing interests and prejudices for the common good, and of emerging from wrack and ruin, sorrow and woe, cleaner mentally and socially than before the sword was drawn.

Wars between great nations seem terrible to mean little men, men meanly brought up and meanly educated, men who can only see great things in a mean little way. But indeed such wars are grand and glorious when compared to the hideous strife of mediæval man, of unorganized mobs, of murderous bullies, and of that great degenerate scum which bubbles up upon the surface of a nation at every crisis. War may be ghastly or sublime ; it is both, but Nature cares neither for the one nor for the other ; she orders evolution, and evolve we must, on her lines and not on those expectorated by some decayed pedagogue. On the lines of war, in which a nation accumulates the wealth of the weak, thus are the strong rewarded ; of peace, in which the strong develop their spoil, thus are the cunning recompensed ; of commercial war, in which the workers accumulate the riches of the masters ; of commercial peace, in which wealth is developed and diffused throughout the world. Peace in decay is more terrible than even a war of wantonness and destruction, as Carlyle so dramatically exclaims :

> " Call ye that a Society, cries he again, where there is no longer any Social Idea extant ; not so much as the Idea of a common Home, but only of a common overcrowded Lodging-house ? Where each, isolated, regardless of his neighbours, clutches what he can get, and cries ' Mine ! ' and calls it Peace, because in the cut-purse and cut-throat scramble, no steel knives, but only a far cunninger sort, can be employed ? "

When this type of peace begins to asphyxiate a nation, it is time to press our swords, however rusty, upon the grindstones of war and cut the throat of the wanton who has deceived us.

As the ethical object of a nation is to gain a moral or common-sense superiority over its neighbours, that is a reputation for honesty and fearlessness in all their many forms, it stands to reason that this objective must be maintained when peace gives way to war, unless ethics are to be cast overboard. Normally, in a healthy nation there should be no break in policy; consequently, in war the policy of rightfulness must be continued without interruption if an ethical profit is to be secured.

In the past, and to a very considerable extent at present, the traditional methods of peace have not been based on a policy of rightfulness but on one of compromise between what nationally is considered good and evil. Most civilized governments have attempted through diplomacy (the object of which should be to guarantee and safeguard peaceful prosperity and honour) to divide the nations which surround them into two categories—future friends and future foes (the good and evil). These categories have then been subjected to a diplomatic bombardment, the former with moralizing impressions and the latter with demoralizing ones. In this bloodless contest the main weapons have been the newspapers of prospective friends and foes, over which frequently controlling interests are obtained. If this unethical process of waging war continues, then, at a near date, we may find that one nation will become the actual owner or hidden controller of another nation's press, and that the words which express the policy of an enemy are thrust down the throats of ignorant people like home-made jam. Words, much more so than thoughts, are omnipotent among crowds, but they must be intelligible, and if the difference originating with Babel can be overcome by an international press, the nation which can control its interests will be in a powerful position to poison the minds of its selected foes. Such action as this I believe to be grossly immoral, and that, in place of its reducing the incidence of war,

5*

it will greatly increase it, especially war in its most disastrous form, namely, civil war.

If this unethical form of diplomacy continue, then it will follow that the grand strategy of the nation, that is the utilization of the national energies for purposes of war, will follow suit. Thus, if it be discovered that a nation's mentality is represented by $10x - 7y$, x representing his possible assets and y his probable deficits, in peace time a prospective adversary might so direct his grand strategy as to reduce x and to increase y. Thus, if one of the x's represents political stability, an unscrupulous nation might attempt to reduce this power for war by sowing seeds of political discord in its competitor's government. If one of the y's be social unrest, it might decide to increase its disruptive influence by stimulating its strength. The first of the means whereby to accomplish this is, as I have already stated, the control of the victim's press, the second the control of the victim's banks. The former constitutes the surest means of disruption and the latter the surest of obtaining information, for, of all records, a nation's pass-books will furnish the most accurate source of information regarding the lives of the leaders of the victim nation, who may, consequently, be blackmailed into declaring war or maintaining peace.

The above processes of corrupting a nation's " will to win " by depriving him of the " power to will " during days of peace are, I affirm, both immoral and Machiavellian, and, worse still, they are foolish, because, in place of enhancing the virtues of a nation which so acts, they render visible its own vices. No man of worth will trust a cheat, a bully, or a cad, however skilful and successful he may be. For a time he may knuckle under, but only to await his chance ; then he will turn on the trickster and rend him, and rightly he will show no mercy. Rightfulness begets mercy in the heart even of a ferocious enemy, and every nation should remember that, in war, it may be defeated, and that, if defeated, according to its past deeds it will be judged and punished.

In spite of the above opinion, war, it must be realized, is not a tourney but a life struggle for existence in which there is no belt which may not be hit under, and, as long as traditional diplomacy exists, this belt will be hit under, for, as I have shown, the ethical objective of war finds its origin in the ethical objective of the nation during the peace which preceded the war. In type, it will follow type, though the tune is played in a higher octave.

Should the ethical outlook of the nation be material and barbarous, so will its actions in war be material and barbarous; consequently, to blame its soldiers for acting materially or brutally is illogical, for they are but the instruments of the policy which has been established by the nation during peace time. The immoralities of war are normally but a continuation of the immoralities of peace. Like an individual soldier or an army, war, as a whole, possesses its moral side, which is the spiritual expression of the accumulated impressions that each individual member of the nation has received during peace time. Consequently, if wars are to be made less barbarous, it is useless restricting the bodily and mechanical activities of the soldier, for these are not ends in themselves. Instead, the spiritual and ethical outlook of the nation must be improved. If war is to be made less brutal, then indeed must philanthropists watch the cradles and the nursery in place of the arsenals and the barrack-room.

Besides the ethical object of the war, viewed as a great national benefit, since time immemorial war has had its traditions and customs which accelerate or retard victory according as their values may be equated in terms of common-sense. Thus, to assassinate prisoners is not so much an immoral act as an uneconomical one. If prisoners are killed off, it will mean that the enemy will fight to the death; that his men will retaliate by killing the prisoners they capture; that the use of prisoners as labourers or hostages will be lost, and that the moral effect of the savagery resulting will upset that cool, deliberate determination which is so necessary in order to control the actions of soldiers on the battlefield. Assassination is, therefore, quite as much a vice in war as in peace. Thus again, the sacking of towns and the killing of civilian inhabitants is wrong, unless these acts can find a commensurate compensation of real military value ; not so much because they entail the loss of property and life, but because they lead to the moral disintegration of an army and sow seeds of hatred which will survive the war.

It must not, however, be forgotten that, while a few years ago, armies alone went forth to battle, to-day entire nations go to war, not only as soldiers but as the moral and material suppliers of soldiers. This being so, we find that, while a short time back, it was clearly possible to differentiate between the military and ethical objectives of nations at war, to-day this differentiation is becoming more and more complex ; so much so, that both these objectives are likely to coincide, and, when this takes place, to attack the civilian workers of a nation will then be as justifiable an act of war as to attack its soldiers.

The ethical traditions of war have little to do with the paper customs and usages manufacturered by elderly and talkative busy-bodies in the quietude of philanthropic debate, but much with unwritten acts of chivalry which refine the brutality of the art. Many of these acts survive to grow into shibboleths which become astringents to victory. Others, more stable in nature, prove true solvents of future difficulties, and these, as might be expected, are based on common-sense. Chivalry, in the broadest meaning of the word, is the cultivation of respect in an enemy for or by his opponent. Outstanding acts of courage, of courtesy, of humanity, give birth to a feeling of superiority or inferiority according as one side excels or falls short of the other. This feeling of superiority, of *noblesse oblige*, is purely ethical, yet it forms the basis of the physical superiority which victory demands. The side which, in war, first attains a superiority in chivalry is the side which attains a spiritual victory over its enemy, a victory which normally not only precedes a material success but which wins the ethical objective of war, which is the true foundation of the peace which follows it.

These acts of chivalry are to a great extent individual acts based on the individual culture of the race. An army of gaol-birds, however well disciplined it may be, will, on the battlefield revert to type directly restraint is released ; so also will an army of cultured men ; but the difference between these two types is, that while in the former case the soldier reverts to a criminal, in the latter he usually continues as an honourable man, for honour is part of his permanent status. On individual acts of honour is chivalry founded.

In many respects war may be compared to a game. It has its rules, which are elastic enough to be of general application ; but there is this difference: While in a game the referee is represented by a third party, a disinterested judge, in war there is no third party, the referee being replaced by the conscience of the combatants themselves. As I have already remarked, there is no belt which may not be hit under ; nevertheless, though this be the case, a wise fighter will think twice before hitting below a certain moral line, because the tactical advantage accruing may be cancelled out by the ethical loss resulting. If in a game of football, however, the referee abscond, and one side, arming itself with sticks, assails the other, it would be ethically and competitively wrong if the side so attacked did not protect itself. Ethically so because brutality would usually triumph ; competitively, because the unarmed side would inevitably be driven from the field. In such circumstances common-sense again holds final judgment, as it always must ; and when, in its accepted forms of chivalry, it can no longer be applied, then application must be sought for through any and every means which will wipe out the insult of a dishonourable opposition. Men who take on the nature of vermin must be exterminated, and in their extermination is the entire moral progress of mankind moved one step nearer its final and unknown goal. To refuse to use base means against a base foe is to set a premium on crime, and in war there are crimes as well as honours. To tolerate crime is neither to act chivalrously towards a criminal or chivalrously towards oneself ; it is the act of a fool, that is of a man who values his self-preservation at the price of a custom which ceasing to be marketable has become counterfeit.

Ultimately, from acts of chivalry on the battlefield do we soar to those acts which form the ethics of grand strategy, the fuller meaning of which I will discuss in Chapter XI. To damage a nation morally during days of peace is not good enough ; it is but a poor endeavour, which normally must bring but little profit. Ethically, during war, as I will show, grand strategy does aim at demoralizing the enemy, yet also does it consist in the enhancement of a nation's worth in the eyes of its actual or potential enemies. Integrity, honour, justice and courage are the weapons of the grand strategist, which not only demonstrate a nation's moral worth but its martial power. The cultivation of these in peace time forms the backbone of success in war.

As long as war is looked upon as a calamity, a kind of international influenza, so long will the true ethics of war be obscured. Up to the present it has been of necessity calamitous, for the means of waging war have been means of destruction, though these means have shown a steady improvement since the days when primitive man wielded the flint axe. I will show, I hope quite clearly, that modern science has now placed at the disposal of the soldier means which it was totally impossible to make use of a few years ago, and that these means will humanize war and raise it from its present barbarous footing to a higher ethical position. While, in the past, because in war men had to be killed, no civilized soldier has suggested that, consequently, nations through their peace policy should aim at secret assassination ; so I believe that, in the future, when it is realized that the most humane method of waging war is the moral attack on the enemy's nerves, no civilized soldier will suggest that the peace policy of war should be based on international terror. This may be the method of atavistic revolutionaries, social throwbacks to the days of Nero, but I fervently hope that they will not be countenanced by soldiers or sane politicians.

For these views to be accepted by armies, there must be a radical change in their political and military mentality. New ideas must be considered freely, criticized freely and judged publicly, and if found more profitable than existing ones—accepted. When in a normally healthy family a child is born, the parents are not only congratulated but are proud and pleased at the event. When, however, in an army some unfortunate in-dividual gives birth to a new idea, he is execrated, and why? Because any new idea is apt to disturb the vested interests and prejudices which bulk so large in military organization. It is the old question of creative thought, the irresistible force, seeking for a niche in the stable opinions which surround it. It is again the old question of the selection of the fittest by means of a struggle between fit and unfit.

The idea is the child of circumstances; it does not spring fully armed from a single head, but is engendered in this head by the rottenness of its surroundings. It is by observing rottenness that purity, or improvement, arises; consequently, the lustiness of the rottenness is very natural, for rottenness is also striving to endure.

When we glance through military history, we find that most new ideas, which eventually materialize into theories or concrete form, originate in piratical exploits outside the existing military organization, and that only after a period of virulent abuse do they become adjuncts or undesirable foster-children in the military family.

The idea proves its value and its champions exaggerate its powers. Opinion now accepts the idea under the covering fire of an offensive directed against the exaggerations. The idea is attached to the traditional elements and begins to consume them, until from the ashes of the old organization arises a new, which usually proves that the exaggerations fall totally short of the full development of the idea. Everyone is now contented; the originators of the idea because they have actually outstepped their predictions; the old school also, for, after all, were not these predictions incorrect? Circumstances having proved them to have fallen sadly short of the mark. The new idea, consequently, is accepted, and, under the new school, which step by step adopts the mentality of the old school, stabilizes, and in its turn has to be broken up by another volcanic eruption.

It is now my intention in the remaining ten Chapters of this book to place a few new ideas before the reader, so that he may judge whether present-day military, naval and air force organizations are the best in order to maintain or enforce policy, and if not, whether my suggestions are better or worse. If better, then I trust that he will support them, for our present defence forces are costing £150,000,000 a year.

IV

THE LAST LAP OF THE PHYSICAL EPOCH

IN this Chapter I intend examining the nature and character of the Great War of 1914–1918, and to show that, tactically, it was based on a gigantic misconception of the true purpose of war, which is to enforce the policy of a nation *at the least cost to itself and enemy* and, consequently, to the world, for so intricately are the resources of civilized states interwoven that to destroy any one country is simultaneously to wound all other nations.

In August, 1914, it cannot be said that the armies of Europe were unprepared for war; they were prepared, and to the proverbial last gaiter button. But for what kind of war, this is the crucial question?

Ever since 1866 and 1870, the eyes of the General Staffs of Europe had been blinded by the brilliance of von Moltke's strategy. Soldiers had gazed on the bayonet points of Sadowa and Sedan until they were hypnotized by these great battles, and, under the influence of this hypnosis, they dreamt of the next war as an immense 1870 operation involving unlimited slaughter.

Their doctrine was founded on two tremendous fallacies. First, that policy is best enforced by destruction; secondly, that military perfection is based on numbers of soldiers. They did not realize that Sadowa and Sedan were won by the weapons of 1866 and 1870. That these weapons had long been replaced by more effective ones. That during the forty years following the capitulation of Paris, science, industry and means of transport had revolutionized the civilized nations of the world. Not realizing this vast change in the conditions which would surround the next war, and meditating on war as a thing in itself, as an end rather than as a means towards an end, the General Staffs of Europe calculated the respective strengths of their armies in tons of human flesh. Then, in 1914, these armies marched after phantoms which, like will-o'-the-wisps, led them to the slaughter-houses of the Grand Couronné, the Marne, Aisne, and Ypres, and, at length, to a partial realization that war is a living art, a system of knowledge and action which must be fed on the civil sciences and nurtured on the civil industries in order to maintain its strength and purpose—the enforcement of a nation's policy with the least detriment to the peace which must follow final victory.

In their conservatism and lethargy armies are indeed extraordinary organizations. Browsing through peace time, like human cattle they are slaughtered during war. So constituted that ability has the greatest difficulty to struggle to the top, the selection of the fittest to command has seldom a refining influence on their constitutions; consequently, when a great Captain does arise, irrespective of the circumstances which surrounded his successes, his system, even if he has no system, is turned into an infallible doctrine, a dogma which becomes a millstone. Marshal Saxe, from whose works I have already quoted, realized this full well when he wrote:

> " Gustavus Adolphus invented a method which was followed by his scholars and carried into execution with great success; but since his time there has been a gradual decline amongst us, which must be imputed to our having blindly adopted maxims, without any examination of the principles on which they are founded; . . . from whence it appears that our present practice is nothing more than a passive compliance with customs, the grounds of which we are absolute strangers to."

Such was the military outlook before the Seven Years' War, and such was the military outlook in July, 1914.

From 1870 onwards, a new civilization had arisen in Europe, based on the enormous growth of railways and the facilities rendered possible by the motor car and lorry. Soldiers had studied these means, not in order to mechanicalize armies, that is to replace muscular by mechanical power, but from the point of view that these means of movement would enable an enemy's frontier to be submerged under a veritable inundation of flesh. Millions of men would sweep forward and, like immense clouds of locusts, would gain victory by sheer weight of numbers. This doctrine was so simple ; moreover the railway appeared to render it possible. Hence the horde armies of 1914.

The strategist had, however, forgotten the tactician. No man could control such vast numbers of men, which, in France, formed two great human stop-butts. This was a colossal error, but not the biggest, for the strategist and the tactician both forgot human nature.

The supreme duty of the soldier is to fight and not to die. As, in 1914, armies could not live on the surface of the battlefield, there was no choice but to go under the surface ; consequently, trenches five hundred miles long were dug, and armies, like foxes, went to earth ; because, since 1870, the magazine rifle, the machine gun and the quick-firing field cannon had replaced the weapons of that day. Consequently, the tactics of Sedan had been rendered quite obsolete—almost as obsolete as the electrical sciences of 1870 would be if compared to those of 1914.

In order to secure these trenches from surprise attack, each side turned itself into an immense spider, and spun around its entrenchments hundreds of thousands of miles of steel web— the common commercial article known as barbed wire, miles of which had been used in South Africa, in 1901, and hundreds of miles of it in the defences of Port Arthur, in 1904. But these wars, especially the latter, though closely studied by soldiers, were examined through 1870 spectacles, and their tactical lessons were blurred through strategical study. Yet one man at least, though not a soldier, did clearly see what the influence of modern weapons on the traditional methods would lead to. This man was Mr. I. S. Bloch, a banker in Warsaw, who, in 1897, published a book in six volumes on " The War of the Future." At the time

soldiers derided Mr. Bloch's ideas and deductions; a wiser procedure would have been to have read his work and to have
absorbed a little knowledge.   In the English translation of the
last volume, which was published in 1899 under the title " Is War
Impossible," Mr. Bloch writes :

> " At first there will be an increased slaughter—increased slaugh-
> ter on so terrible a scale as to render it impossible to get troops to
> push the battle to a decisive issue.   They will try to, thinking
> that they are fighting under the old conditions, and they will learn
> such a lesson that they will abandon the attempt for ever.   Then,
> instead of a war fought out to the bitter end in a series of decisive
> battles, we shall have as a substitute a long period of continually
> increasing strain upon the resources of the combatants.   The war,
> instead of being a hand-to-hand contest, in which the combatants
> measure their physical and moral superiority, will become a kind of
> stalemate, in which, neither army being willing to get at the other,
> both armies will be maintained in opposition to each other, threaten-
> ing the other, but never being able to deliver a final and decisive
> attack. . . . That is the future of war—not fighting, but famine,
> not the slaying of men, but the bankruptcy of nations and the
> break-up of the whole social organization. . . . Everybody will
> be entrenched in the next war.   It will be a great war of entrench-
> ments.   The spade will be as indispensable to a soldier as his
> rifle. . . . All wars will of necessity partake of the character of
> siege operations. . . . Your soldiers may fight as they please;
> the ultimate decision is in the hands of famine. . . ."

The above constitutes an accurate forecast of events in
1914–1917, which were rehearsed ten years previously, on a
smaller scale, at Nan Shan, Liao Yang and Mukden.   Their
deduction was a matter of pure common-sense.   Given a magazine
rifle firing ten aimed rounds a minute, a machine gun firing
five hundred rounds and a field gun firing ten rounds, even in
1904 it was beyond question that the tactics of 1870 were as
unsuited to twentieth century weapons as the machine tools
of an 1870 workshop would be unsuited to a twentieth century
manufactory.   In connection with this criticism, which I believe
to be sound, though possibly unpalatable, I will hazard to quote
two personal experiences.   In April, 1914, when a student at
the Camberley Staff College, I had occasion to visit an Artillery

Practice Camp at Larkhill (Salisbury Plain), and so struck was I by the power of the quick-firing field gun that I wrote the following :

> "The leading lesson which I learnt whilst at this camp only accentuated what reading had already led me to suppose, namely, that artillery is to-day the superior arm, and that, consequently, battles will become more static, i.e., entrenched. That its power is so great that the infantry assault will be chiefly rendered possible by the demoralization of the enemy by means of artillery fire. This logically leads to penetration in place of envelopment as the grand tactical principle of the attack, because freedom of manœuvre will be limited by wire and field works ; to an enormous expenditure of ammunition at the decisive point, and to consideration whether a special motor ammunition column should not be formed to supply alone the guns taking part in the decisive artillery attack."

This deduction was not accepted.

During the same month I wrote a memoir on the tactics of penetration* in which I considered the tactics of the next war. In it I said :

> "To-day we have, besides the magazine-rifle, the characteristics of which are understood, two, comparatively speaking, new weapons : the quick-firing field gun and the machine gun. Realizing this, we can predict with absolute certainty that the general who makes the truest use of these weapons, that is so deploys his men that their fullest power is attained, will win, unless he is hopelessly outnumbered. If this general further devise a system of deployment which will not only accentuate the power of these weapons, but also the defects in his opponent's formation, he will win irrespective of numbers, as surely as 1,400 Swiss beat 15,000 Austrians at Mortgarten, and as surely as 90,000 Austrians were beaten by 33,000 Prussians at Leuthen. This is a certainty.
>
> "From 1840 to the close of the nineteenth century, improvements steadily forced the rifle to the fore. A similar progress did not take place in the manufacture of cannon, breech-loading guns not being finally adopted by the British Army until 1886. By the beginning of the present century we find the rifle master of all it surveyed ; machine guns were being still used experimentally, trajectories were slightly more curved than to-day, indirect laying was only exceptionally employed ; but of all the changes intro-

---

* Published in November, 1914, in the Journal of the Royal United Service Institution under the title "The Tactics of Penetration. A Counterblast to German Numerical Superiority."

duced since the Russo-Japanese war, the general adoption of quick-firing artillery by civilized armies is out and out the greatest. This gun, if correctly employed, will, I feel, revolutionize the present theory of war by substituting as the leading grand tactical principle penetration for that of envelopment.

      *   *   *   *   *   *   *   *

" To-day, on account of the rapidity of fire of the modern field gun, there will be no necessity either to hold back guns in reserve, or to withdraw them from their positions, for all that will be necessary will be to mass ammunition opposite a definite point, or a topographically weak point, or a point which has become or is likely to become a decisive point, so that the guns commanding this point, few or many in number, may pour a continuous and terrific deluge of shells on this point, and so enable the decisive attack to proceed against it. Admitting that this is feasible, then the problem resolves itself into one of supplying these breaching batteries with sufficient ammunition ; this problem should not be a difficult one to solve now that motor transport is in general use.

" If I am right in this deduction, then I am right in adding : that that side which can first throw its adversary on the defensive, and, by so doing, can select at will the decisive point of attack—or which can, through a careful study of the ground, foresee this decisive point, or any moderately weak point—has all to gain by so doing. The defence cannot gauge, or will have the greatest difficulty in gauging, even by means of aerial reconnaissance, the point against which the decisive attack is going to be launched if the assailants' preparatory attack be violently offensive. All it can do is to attempt to take the attack, or assault, in flank, just as the 52nd Regiment took the Old Guard of Napoleon in flank at the close of the Battle of Waterloo, or as Colonel Daubeney, in his astonishing charge at Inkerman, cut the great Russian trunk column in two as it neared the Home Ridge."

I then examined the dangers of the above proposals and suggested the use of the machine gun in order to lessen them. I wrote :

" There is as much difference between machine-gun and infantry fire to-day as there was between light infantry and heavy infantry fire a hundred years ago. So great is this difference that we might almost say that the light infantry of the future will be evolved from the machine gunners of the present. That is that the assaulting column of the future will be flanked by these terror-spreading weapons, and that these new light infantrymen, like the old, will not only precede the assaulting column by working up close to the line of the holding attack, but will flank it on both sides, producing a somewhat similar effect on the hostile line as grape, canister and case shot did during the first fifty years of the last century."

I concluded this memoir by saying :

"I have no doctrine to preach, for I believe in none. Every concrete case demands its own particular solution, and for this solution all that we require is skill and knowledge, skill in the use of our weapons, knowledge of our enemy's formations.

"A physician who is slave to a doctrine, as was the famous Doctor Sangrado in 'Gil Blas,' ends by killing his patients ; a general who is under the spell of some such shibboleth as the oblique-order, envelopment, penetration, or the *offensive à outrance*, ends by destroying his army. There is no difference. If there is a doctrine at all, then it is common-sense, that is, action adapted to circumstances.

"I do not lay down that I am right in basing my proposed deployment for penetration principally on the power of quick-firing artillery ; but all I can say is this : that a careful study of past and present history has led me to the following conclusions :

(1) "That weapons when correctly handled seldom fail to gain victory.

(2) "That armies are more often ruined by dogmas springing from their former successes than by the skill of their opponents. . . ."

The criticism on this memoir was : "Lacking in sound military judgment."

I must offer the reader an apology for the introduction of so much personal matter, and I must ask him to believe me when I say that I have not done this in order to pat my prevision on the back, but to show that it is possible for a soldier, possessing a normal standard of intelligence, to be wise *before* the event. So frequently have I been told how easy is it to be wise *after* the event (which is surely better than never being wise at all), that I have quoted the above extracts from my writings, extracts containing military opinons which, though imperfect, were not lacking in sound military judgment, as the history of the war testifies, in order that such of my readers who are not altogether blinded by tradition may have some confidence in the new ideas contained in this book. I do not ask them to swallow

these ideas whole, but I do ask them not to proclaim them
indigestible before mentally they have tasted them.   I will now
return to the magical year—1866.

From the battle of Sadowa onwards, tactical envelopment
became a shibboleth, and any idea of defensive warfare a heresy.
Not that envelopment in itself is not an admirable manœuvre,
but that its effectiveness depends on circumstances, the conditions
of the moment under which the principles of war have to be
applied.   So also is the offensive a military virtue, but this in
no way means that the defensive is a military vice.

In August, 1914, the German armies were drawn up in phal-
angial formation from Aachen to Basle.   Their right was to
wheel through Belgium, round Paris, and then advance eastwards,
sweeping the armies of France into Germany and Switzerland.
This plan was extraordinarily simple and the railways appeared
to render it possible.   It was so simple that the German General
Staff were apparently of the opinion, as their system of promotion
did not guarantee their possessing a skilled leader when war
broke out, that genius could be replaced by mechanical movement ; in other words, that the goose step could replace intellect !
The unexpected was expunged ; consequently, a reserve to meet
it was unnecessary.   They violated the principles of concentration
and economy of force, and sealed their fate by so doing.

The French General Staff must have realized the extreme
likelihood of the German right wing marching through Belgium.
Bearing this in mind, where then should their reserve army have
been ?   At Paris, because Paris is the biggest railway centre in
north-eastern France.   Where were their reserves ?   Near Verdun !   Even if the Germans had restricted their front of attack to
the line Thionville-Basle, the best position of the French reserves
was Paris ; even if they had proceeded by sea and disembarked
their armies at Cherbourg, Brest or Bordeaux ; even if they had
landed them at Toulon or marched through Italy or Switzerland,
the *only* strategic position for the reserves was Paris !   Why
were the reserves near Verdun ?   Because, after the crushing
defeats sustained by the French armies in 1870, this staff had

turned to that oracle of modern warfare—Napoleon, and in his wars had sought an answer to the problem of future victory. In his many campaigns, they discovered that he frequently made use of a lozenge formation—an advanced guard, two strong wings and a central reserve. Here then was the secret of success. So they drew up their plan accordingly, forgetting that, in the days of Napoleon, railways did not exist, and that, consequently, his reserves were so placed as to be within easy marching distance of the other forces. Had the French General Staff done what Napoleon, in the strategical circumstances which railways had created, could scarcely have failed to do—concentrate every available man at Paris, wait, see and spring, instead of the French Armies being swept into Switzerland, the whole of the German right wing would have been annihilated and, quite possibly, the war would have been won in six weeks.

" It is the MAN, not men who count in war," once said Napoleon. I will add to this aphorism : such a man does not turn his brain into a museum for past battles—for the only war for him is the next war !

Once the first great operation of the war—the German envelopment of the French armies, had been frustrated by the counter-attack of the Allies during the latter stages of that series of battles known as the battle of the Marne, equilibrium was established on the slopes of the river Aisne. This condition was followed by a race to the coast and culminated in the defeat of the Germans at the first battle of Ypres, at which battle traditional warfare on the Western Front terminated. Henceforth for several years the war on this front was destined to become a war of entrenchments, a siege, and the main weapon in the armoury of the besieger is famine.

Meanwhile, at sea another war was in progress, a war but distantly connected with the land operations except for one incident which in fact constituted the most astonishing naval operation of the war.

On August 4, 1914, two German warships, the *Goeben* and *Breslau*, were busily engaged in taking in supplies at Messina

6*

They could not escape through the Straits of Gibraltar nor through the Suez Canal. They could either seek refuge in Pola or in the Sea of Marmora. Of these two lines of retreat, the first was objectless, the second full of possibilities; consequently, Admiral Souchon adopted the second line and sailed for the Dardanelles, through which he steamed on August 10. In England this astute move was derided, because the greatest naval power in the world could only think traditionally of naval warfare. Ships as fighting machines were understood, but as political instruments —no! such use was beyond the traditional ken. Out of the *Goeben* sprouted the Gallipoli campaign, and out of its failure the Middle East Problem. What a move: for the West, the most decisive since Trafalgar.

While, prior to the war, in the great armies of the world, we find man-power obliterating tactics, so in the great navies do we find machine-power doing exactly the same thing. Men and more men, battleships and more battleships, but how these men or battleships should fight or be fought, and what influence the inventions of the last forty years would have on tactics was not even imagined. On land, soldiers were expected to fight much as they fought in 1870, and at sea sailors would fight much as they fought in 1805. Such was the position in 1914. Well might Admiral Mahan write:

> " The student will observe that changes in tactics have not only taken place *after* changes in weapons, which necessarily is the case, but that the interval between such changes has been unduly long. This doubtless arises from the fact that an improvement of weapons is due to the energy of one or two men, while changes in tactics have to overcome the inertia of a conservative class; but it is a great evil. It can be remedied only by a candid recognition of each change."

So conservative had the naval mind become that, in 1914, it had not fully realized the greatest of all modern influences on sea fighting—the replacement of wind by steam as a means of fleet propulsion. The doctrine of fleet tactics, as held in July, 1914, was in brief: " parallel actions with a hope of envelopment." These actions to be fought at what to-day would appear to be ridiculously short ranges.

The moral influence of the unknown factors of modern naval warfare—the realization of the conditions under which the objective had to be gained ; the power of weapons the nature of which was not fully understood, and lack of knowledge in tactics, consequent on this ignorance, were due not so much to inefficiency as to the fact that mechanical progress had outstepped tactical thought and training. Time, in fact, had been insufficient wherein to digest science, and the result was that, while the grand tactical purpose of the opposing fleets had been based on decisive action during peace time, directly war was declared the unknown quantities, the resultants of science, materialized, and the war at sea, like the war on land, assumed a deadlock, attrition replacing the offensive as the grand tactics of the opposing sides.

Thus we see that, when we examine the opening phases of the Great War, traditionally educated and trained armies and navies have but one chance of success, that is the initial operation they undertake. Success being based on the fact that as their opponents may also be tradition-bound, their own tradition may triumph over that of their adversaries. Also we see that, if the initial clash of arms does not result in victory, at once the influence of weapons, means of movement and protection, which have been designed since these traditions became stabilized in blind custom and routine, exert their sway and bring traditional warfare to an end, and out of the knowledge gained from these weapons slowly evolves a new doctrine which replaces the old dogma.

Throughout the Great War, we watch this struggle between the new and the old. The old cannot imagine that its dogma is wrong : was not it successful in 1870, and has not it been laid down in every manual and text book since ? The new scoffs and exaggerates ; it is carried away by its own novelty, which gains an unnatural brilliance by being contrasted with the opaque substance of dead thought. When we examine the military history of the late Middle Ages, it astonishes us to watch the Chivalry of France being, for the space of a century, mown down by arrows and still not grasping the tactical value of the bow.   In years to come, some future historian may possibly contrast, with this suicidal adherence to custom, the fact that, though in 1904 the machine gun had proved itself to be the most deadly of small-arm weapons, ten years later the great armies of Europe had to learn this lesson again.   In fact it would appear that both soldier and sailor possess no power of absorbing tactical knowledge except through personal experience.   In 1899 a British Division was equipped with twenty-four machine guns ; in 1914 it was still equipped with twenty-four : yet, in 1918, fearful cost in life had compelled the number of automatic weapons to be increased to over five hundred.   Accepting this number as necessary, why was the 1914 equipment the same as that of 1899 ?   The answer is, it had become a tradition that the number of machine guns in a battalion should be two ; just as in the fourteenth century it was a tradition that no gentleman could fight save on horseback.

The objective in war may, as the text books declare, be the imposition of the will of one army on the other, yet history shows that the purpose of an army or navy has, in peace time, little to do with war, its object being not freely to evolve but in place to maintain its traditions.   Some are vital to its existence, others full of the germs of decay.   Both are, however, holy, and to attack either is military blasphemy.   I will now turn to the next period of the Great War — the attack by matériel.

After a few weeks of *real* warfare, the *offensive à outrance*, that high gospel of the pre-war manuals, was reduced to a wallowing defensive among mud holes and barbed wire.   Armies, through their own lack of foresight, were reduced to the position of human cattle.   They browsed behind their fences, and on occasion snorted and bellowed at each other.   The one problem which now confronted them was : how to re-establish movement, for until one or both sides could move there was no possibility of a decision by arms, and famine alone must become the arbiter of peace. Some there were who actually recommended this course, but their voices were drowned by shouts for shells. Shells were to be the panacea of all difficulties, more shells and still more shells, and then by steel a road could be blasted to Paris or Berlin. A veritable blood and iron lust swept over the armies of Europe.

As the entire arsenals of the civilized world could not possibly meet the demand, the General Staffs turned to the industries of their respective nations, and a new battle was begun. Which nation would produce the largest output ? For on this output, so it was thought, would victory depend. Of all great industrial countries, Great Britain was the least well prepared for this engagement, because the true meaning of the quick-firing gun had not been grasped. Nevertheless, the astonishing ability for improvisation possessed by Englishmen enabled them so well to cope with the supply, that the General Staff literally became intoxicated on T.N.T. We now lose sight of strategy and tactics in a storm of shells and roaring high explosives; our very tympanums are rent !

For the preliminary bombardments of the battle of Hooge, we fired 18,000 shells; for those at the battle of the Somme, 2,000,000 shells, for those at Arras, in 1917, 2,000,000 shells, and for those at Ypres the same year, 4,300,000 shells. At the last-mentioned battle the tonnage of shells fired during the preliminary bombardments alone amounted to 107,000 tons, the cost of which has been estimated at £22,000,000, a figure very nearly equal to the total yearly cost of the pre-war British Home Army. If this enormous expenditure had resulted in victory, to the traditional soldier it would have been cheap at the price. But it did not result in victory, and it could not result in victory, and for the following very simple reason. In the process of digging up trenches by means of shell fire, everything in the neighbourhood of the trenches was dug up. Roads vanished, tracks vanished, railways vanished and the surface of the ground vanished under the influence of the material earthquake to which all things were subjected. The enemy was killed, his wire entanglements were cut to pieces and his trenches were blown in. Yet in these very acts of destruction was an impassable crater area formed, and, when surface water abounded, as at Ypres, or when rain fell in torrents, as at Beaumont Hamel, none save water-fowl could have crossed the morass of mud, and then these birds would have done better to fly. In place of accelerating infantry movement, every shell that fell impeded this all necessary act of winning the war by force of arms.

There was another reason, and a more visible one still, why this monstrous attack by shells was doomed to failure when directed against a well-organized antagonist, namely, that bombardments lasting from seven to twenty-one days in duration rendered any form of surprise impossible. When a big game hunter visits East Africa to shoot lions, he does not equip himself with a bassoon, and then, when a lion is met with, walk round the beast for a fortnight playing on this instrument. He does not thus comport himself, since all idea of surprise would vanish, and so also would the lion. Unfortunately, a staunch and determined enemy does not behave like a wild animal, in place of bolting from the bassoon, he assembles his forces opposite the spot which is being, like Jericho, trumpeted to earth, and, when the attack is well bogged in the slough created by gun-fire, attacks in his turn. That our great artillery battles killed thousands of Germans is undoubted, they could not help doing so, but equally is it certain that they resulted in terrific casualties to ourselves. The battles on the Somme, in 1916, and at Ypres, in 1917, cost the British Army in killed, wounded and missing, over 800,000 casualties, and as we were the attackers, the probabilities are that our casualties were considerably heavier than those of the Germans. Also is it asserted that these battles were of assistance in beating the enemy, that they used up the enemy's fighting forces and accelerated demoralization : but it may well be asked—at what price ?

In my own opinion, the monopoly of strategy and tactics by shell bludgeoning prolonged the war in place of shortening it. It dulled the imagination of the higher command, who became obsessed by two ideas : fill the trenches to hold them, and blow them to pieces to capture them. Consequently, we see during this period, which was a long one, the art of war slipping back to the position it held in the days of the Macedonian phalanx. As the brain power of the opposing armies grew smaller, for all General Staffs fell victims to the shell-plague, the bodies of these same armies grew bigger and bigger, until the administrative organization for the supply of matériel alone absorbed such vast numbers of men that, through shortage of man-power, the fighting troops were nearly strangled by those whose duty it was to administer to their needs—armies had now become pot-bellied and pea-brained.

The completeness of the deadlock, the seemingly impossible task of re-establishing movement in the decisive theatre of the war, resulted, in a marked extent, in a monopolization of the war plan by amateur political strategists. The war had either to be won, lost, or drawn ; consequently, as the problem on the Western Front was considered unsolvable, some other front had to be discovered. Already, early in 1915, the Germans had changed their main objective. Their intention was no longer to destroy the French armies but the Russian, because of all the armies contending the Russian army was in tactics the least developed, for their traditionalism was very old and very obsolete, and more hidebound than that of France. The giant said : I have 15,000,000 men classified for mobilization ; I have as many infantry divisions as France and Germany put together, and of cavalry beyond number. I will " make up for deficiencies in technique by lavish expenditure of blood ; " and before the war was a year old the Russian casualties totalled just under 4,000,000 ! In 1917, Brusilov's armies lost no less than 375,000 men in twenty-seven days, and about 1,000,000 in four months. All we can do is to gasp at this madness. If war, as it is so often asserted, is a continuation of peace policy, then war is also a link with the policy which will follow victory. During peace, man's policy is to live and not to die : consequently, if war be a continuation of this policy, then soldiers should not be sacrificed like rabbits in an Australian catch.

"The Russians," writes General Knox, "were just big-hearted children who had thought out nothing, and had stumbled half-asleep into a wasps' nest." In nature they were generous, always willing to sacrifice themselves for their allies, in character corrupt, and in disposition childlike. The leadership of their generals was beneath contempt. Just before Tannenberg, General Samsonov sent back for his sword, remarking " that he was now in an enemy's country, and must go armed." His " all prevailing idea was to try and see the battle with his own eyes," *à la* Cossack. Rennenkampf was just as bad ; on one occasion when the Germans withdrew, he said to another officer : " You can take off your clothes now ; the Germans are retiring," quite failing to see that it was the very moment to attack and not to go to bed. Cavalry charged trenches ; the Guards refused to promote ensigns from the ranks, " as men so promoted might remain with them after the war ! " A minister was entitled to draw horse hire per verst for twenty-four horses when, *by rail*, he visited Vladivostock ! And when General Gulevich received a telegram appointing him to an active command, as he at first thought, he was much upset, for it was his custom to rest in bed between two and five p.m. daily. But when he discovered that the appointment was *only* that of Chief of the Staff of the North-West Front he was greatly relieved, and at once gave orders for a thanksgiving service to be held. " Few officers attended this service, for they had all rushed off to scribble memoranda for the General's guidance of the honours and rewards they wished to receive."*

I have made this digression into the internal state of Russian military traditionalism not only to show to what a parlous state of inefficiency stagnation may bring an army, but because it had a pronounced influence on the economic phase of the war. Not only did the deficiencies of the Russian army demand an

* " With the Russian Armies, 1914-1917," Major-General Sir Alfred Knox, K.C.B., C.M.G.

enormous provision of munitions, but they dragged the war eastwards. For the Germans this change of front was comparatively easy ; for us and the French it would have been impossible had we not possessed command of the sea. Thus we watch the military weakness of Russia acting as an incentive to the Germans to close down their operations on the Western Front, and, by means of their magnificent railway system, to reopen operations in Poland. In order to follow suit, the Allies, though knowing full well that the German forces in the West were inferior to their own, followed up this move with an attempt to capture Constantinople, so that, by gaining command of the Black Sea, the Russian armies might be supplied. In truth Russian strength did not lie in supplies, but, as in 1813, in retirement. Thus we see that though these supplies may have added to the moral of the Russian troops, by persuading them not to retire except through force of arms, they prolonged the war. What, I am of opinion, the Russians should have done was what the Germans did on part of the Western Front in February, 1917, that is retire to a Hindenburg line (not necessarily trenches), not a line twenty miles in rear, but two hundred, three hundred, or possibly four hundred.

In the Gallipoli campaign, the abuse of matériel was the main cause of its failure. " In 1906 the possibilities of such an attack had been examined by the British General Staff, and the opinion arrived at was that an unaided action by the fleet was to be deprecated ; and if combined operations were to be undertaken, no landing could be effected on the Gallipoli Peninsula unless the co-operating naval squadron could guarantee with its guns that the landing force should reach the shore unmolested and find after disembarkation a sufficiently extended area, free from hostile fire, to enable it to form up for battle on suitable ground. In summing up, the General Staff stated that they did not consider that the co-operating fleet would be able to give this guarantee, and they recommended such an operation should not be attempted."*

* " Soldiers of the Prophet," Lieut.-Colonel C. C. R. Murphy, p. 121

Though there was only one possible hope of such an attack succeeding, namely, that its initiation should come as a complete surprise, as early as November 3, 1914, the British Navy, by shelling the forts at the entrance of the Dardanelles, first drew the attention of the Turkish General Staff to a theatre of operations which offered decisive results. On March 5, 1915, a further bombardment took place, and on April 25, the first landing was attempted.

In these operations the mistake made by the navy was identical with the mistake which governed the operations of the army during this period in the evolution of the war. Surprise—the moral attack, was replaced by bombardment—the matériel attack ; cunning was ousted by steel, and the attack once again failed.

When considering the phases into which I have divided the war, it must not be supposed that any hard or fast dividing line can be drawn between them. To me they are comparable to a geological chart. The periods—tertiary, quaternary, etc., are shown by well defined bands of colour containing within each drawings of the types of animals, plants and minerals more especially belonging to each epoch. In fact there are no dividing lines, no fixed beginnings or endings, only a slow steady progression. Similarly with the phases of the Great War, which I am now examining : one period emerges from another, takes form, and then falls under the spell of some virile idea which the tests and trials of the war have proved sound. We see this clearly in the increasing employment of the most powerful of the older weapons—quick-firing guns and machine guns ; then of the newer weapons—aeroplanes and submarines, and lastly of altogether new weapons—gas and tanks.

As traditional warfare merges into the war of matériel, every possible effort is made to enhance gun-power by air-power, in the form of fire-control and direction from the air, and yet, as I will show later on, this was not the main duty of the aeroplane. So also with the submarine ; at first she was considered as a minor adjunct of a fleet ; nevertheless, as the war proved, her main power lay in her ability to dispense with fleet protection and to become the sniper of the seas.

As traditional warfare could find no solution to the problem of re-establishing mobility once battle fronts had become entrenched, and as soldiers, for the most part, could only think of war in traditional terms, the solution to this problem had, in the main, to be sought outside normal military thought, and the only place to seek it was among the civil sciences. Being a great chemical country, Germany turned to gas, and being a great engineering country, we, in Great Britain, turned to the petrol engine and produced the tank. The actual date when these two new means of war were first thought of does not much matter, for the ideas underlying them are very old, but a study of modern warfare in general and of modern industry in particular would have given the General Staffs of Europe a clearer idea of the probable nature of the next war than the one held by them in 1914. Unshackled by the traditional aspect of warfare, it was for this reason that Mr. Bloch, a pacifist, was able to visualize the nature of the next war more clearly than the most eminent of General Staff Officers. If it had only been appreciated that, failing an overwhelming initial success, such as a second Sadowa or Sedan, the next war would be a war of trenches, then it would have logically followed that not only would enormous quantities of ammunition be required, but to maintain mobility under the tornado resulting, armour would have to be reintroduced.

The last of the great siege wars was the war in the Crimea, and though this war had been studied by soldiers it had been little understood. Had it been carefully examined, it would have been realized that the conditions of 1915 were very similar to those of 1854, and that the difficulties of 1915 could be overcome by the solutions suggested to meet those which confronted the British Army in 1854.

In 1854, we find Mr. James Cowen, a philanthropist, suggesting to the British Government the adoption of a " locomotive land battery fitted with scythes to mow down infantry " : in other words the tank.   The same year, Lord Dundonald, a noted admiral, suggested that gas could be usefully employed in order to asphyxiate the garrison of Sebastopol.   Neither of these suggestions was adopted, because they did not harmonize with the traditional methods of waging war.   They were considered too terrible to be contemplated.   Curious to relate, however, the government which showed such qualms as regards killing the enemy showed none as regards inflicting a miserable death on thousands of our own men through their gross neglect of administrative arrangements and hospital necessities.   The reason for this was that death by typhus, dysentery and neglected wounds did not violate tradition, while death by gassing or mowing down would have.   In the Crimean war, tradition won through, and at what suffering and cost !

In the Great War, tradition once again formed phalanx against all innovation and improvement ; luckily for us, it went down before the hammer-blows of science, but unfortunately, though expectedly, immediately the Armistice had been signed, tradition rose like a phœnix from its ashes.

For a generation to come, tradition will fight against the new doctrines of warfare.   These will ultimately win through, as they must, and, in the internecine struggle between 1914 and 1918 organizations, will once again the next war be forgotten.   Our only chance to escape this calamity is to change our outlook on history ; in place of solidifying reason, history should liquefy the imagination.   History never actually repeats itself, for it constitutes one continuous transformation.   Its tendencies may be ascertained by study, but foresight into these demands more than study : it demands meditation and a continuous use of the word " why ? "

I will now examine the next great period, that of the economic attack.

The enormous demands made for all types of munitions of war and warlike supplies during the phase of the matériel attack, brought into a clear light those economic foundations of the war which, in peace time, had lain too deep to be noticed much by soldiers. First, these munitions had to be supplied; secondly, their supply curtailed the manufacture of luxuries as well as many everyday necessities. So visible did these economic foundations become, that it was not long before the General Staffs of the contending nations realized that, if the food supply of the enemy could be cut off, the will of the hostile civil population would be undermined, and with this loss of will to endure, their military forces would be rendered useless.

The first military problem of the Allies now became that of the circumvallation of the Central Powers; their second problem, their surrender by starvation. Consequently, during the third phase of the war, the problem of re-establishing tactical mobility was to a certain extent replaced by a direct attack on the enemy's stomach. The nature of this type of war is simple, yet, throughout history, it has been persistently misunderstood.

Starvation is a means towards an end and not the end itself, and I will repeat it again: the end, objective or goal in warfare is the imposition of the policy of one hostile government on another, the foundations of these respective policies being the wills of the contending nations. These wills must, however, be attacked in such a manner that their possessors are not permanently injured; for to weaken the enemy, either permanently or for a long period after the cessation of hostilities, is, as I have already pointed out, tantamount to wounding one's own body by a self-inflicted blow. Such a blow is immoral, not because it compels an enemy to accept a policy which is distasteful to him, but because, by reducing the physique of the enemy and especially of the enemy's children, it ultimately not only reduces his prosperity but the prosperity of the world—it is in fact a blow directed against civilization.

The encirclement of the Central Powers by the Allies resulted in the most gigantic siege in history, the lines of circumvallation running from Calais to Kermanshah, and thence through Russia to the Baltic. The establishment of this immense circle of bayonets took time, but what took longer still was the time taken by the British Government to realize that, once this siege had been determined on, the lines of circumvallation were useless as long as supplies could be shipped in vast quantities to neutral countries and thence transported to Germany. The problem of starvation was virtually a politico-naval one, and the politician was afraid of enforcing it, not because it was immoral, but because it might prove detrimental to the pockets of neutrals who, like vampires, were feasting on the blood of the battlefields. Such neutrality as this is beneath contempt, and during the war its immorality was only exceeded by the vice of political fear.

The bottling up of the German fleet immediately after the declaration of war drew the attention of the German Government to the necessity of economy in resources, especially of all food stocks. In December, 1914, Professor Eltzbacher produced a book on this subject entitled : " Die deutsche Volksernährung und der englische Aushungerungsplan,"* which dealt with this question in minute detail down to the tonnage of dog's flesh. Outside scientific circles, however, little attention was paid to this question in England, as may be gathered from Professor Poulton's " Romanes Lecture " for 1915. In this lecture he says :

> " Lord Robert Robert Cecil is reported in *The Times* of December 3rd (1915) to have said, ' Our policy was to secure our rights and to starve Germany first of all. Starving Germany was, of course, only a metaphorical expression—it was impossible ; he would rather say deprive her of essential articles.' What right had Lord Robert to say that the starving of Germany was impossible ? He is not an expert on food supply, and he quoted no authority. Has he studied the Eltzbacher memoirs and Dr. Waller's and Professor Ashley's criticisms ? Has he asked for a report from the Royal Society's Committee on the food supply of Germany ? What we really need to end this war is *knowledge* and firm action based on it. As it is, with the slipshod ways of conducting war and neglect of scientific authority, our own Government has done very much to help Germany out of the difficulty. It has ignored, as Dr. Waller says in the introduction to the English translation, ' the obvious fact that the food of a besieged nation, as of a besieged fortress, in

---

* English edition 1915, " Germany's Food and England's Plan to starve Her out."

tons of bread, meat and potatoes is as truly its ammunition as are its shells.' "*

From the above we see that while the War Office and the Admiralty were exerting all their strength to encircle and so besiege the Central Powers, the Board of Trade was forcibly feeding these Powers through the Dutch spout. Neutral countries may possess certain rights during war time, but to allow them to supply the enemy with food when he is being besieged is to turn even traditional warfare upside-down.

When, however, the blockade began to tighten, Germany had no intention of committing *felo-de-se* in order to maintain a naval custom or a humanitarian tradition. She was now fighting for her life, and not being able to hit above the belt she hit below it in order to make good by cunning her physical naval deficit. She was, consequently, outlawed. Though the infringement of international rules and customs is always dangerous, as it enables an adversary to call the kettle black, Germany, in my opinion, in the circumstances in which the blockade placed her, was justified in her turn in attempting to establish a blockade of her enemies' coast-lines by the unrestricted use of the submarine. If this action was an infringement of international law and the (fictitious) rights of neutrals, then those neutral countries which were affected should have supported their rights by declaring war on the law-breaker. In place, most of these weedlings howled with injured innocence and continued to make money out of the battlefields they were too prudent or too cowardly to approach. There can be no doubt that, by instituting unrestricted submarine warfare, the Germans violated certain laws of war made long before the advent of this weapon ; but also can there be no doubt that, if the slow starvation of German men, women and children by means of investment did not contravene the spirit of international

* " Science and the Great War," E. B. Poulton, D.Sc., M.A., pp 31-32. In December, 1913, Holland imported 1⅛ million tons of cocoa ; in December, 1914, imports in cocoa rose to 7¼ million tons. On account of the abnormal tonnage of oranges sent to Germany " on the Empress's birthday every German soldier was presented with a pot of marmalade ! "

law, then neither did unrestricted submarine warfare contravene it, though it may have infringed the letter of the tradition which this law had created. If starvation is right in one case it is right in both. The drowning of non-combatants is but an incident in the operation of killing by starvation, it does not affect the principle underlying this act. Further, it should be realized that, as long as international law is so worded as to permit of neutrals trading like ghouls on the blood of the belligerents, international law is immoral and, consequently, it is a virtuous act to destroy it. To foster it is not only to place a premium on greed and cowardice but also on moral prostitution.

During the period of the economic attack, the whole question of the security of property on the high seas was thrown into the limelight. This question is an old one, and a very brief summary of its history is instructive.

Up to the middle of the fourteenth century, capture at sea was practically unrestricted. Then we find several of the leading European nations binding themselves by an agreement known as the " Consolat-del-Mar," in which it was laid down that only enemy property, either ships or cargo, was liable to capture and that neutral ships and cargo were not. During the Crimean War, both Great Britain and France agreed not to capture enemy's goods in neutral ships or neutral goods in enemy ships. In 1856, Great Britain became party to the Declaration of Paris, and hung a millstone round her neck by agreeing to exempt from capture enemy's goods in neutral ships and neutral goods in enemy ships, subject to the exception of contrabands. In 1871 Lord Salisbury said: " Since the Declaration of Paris the fleet, valuable as it is for preventing an invasion of these shores, is almost valueless for any other purpose," and shortly before the outbreak of war, in 1914, Major J. A. Longridge wrote:

" The Declaration of Paris curtails the offensive power of the only weapon with which, in the absence of an army of continental proportions, she (i.e. Great Britain) can make good her word when she speaks with her enemies in the gate."*

* " The Liability of Forfeiture of National Oversea Commerce," Major J. A. Longridge. " The Army Review," Vol. VI., April, 1914.

If sufficient harm had not already been accomplished by depriving the fleet of an economic objective, shortly before the war, the British Government contemplated a further restriction of her naval powers by considering very favourably the terms of the Declaration of London ; fortunately for the Empire this Declaration was still unratified when hostilities began.

From the opening of the war onwards, few opportunities of a surreptitious nature were missed by Great Britain to file through the shackles of the Declaration of Paris, and when we view these attempts from an impartial point of view, there can be little doubt that, technically at least, Germany was right in stating that we had violated the terms of this Declaration, and that, consequently, she in her turn was free to torpedo ships at sight. Here, again, can we learn another lesson concerning the dangers of rules based on pseudo-humanitarian vapourings. The Declaration of Paris was a pacifical measure adopted to restrict the horrors of war ; it was not based on common-sense or human nature, and what happened was pre-ordained. Having agreed to it in peace time, Great Britain tried to wriggle out of it in war time, with the inevitable result that Germany made these wriggles an excuse to institute a form of warfare which was, from the standpoint of the signatories of the Declaration, more barbarous than any type of warfare yet contemplated.

In the German economic campaign, one cardinal military error was made—it was declared too early. Had the Germans delayed their declaration until the end of 1917, and then launched an unrestricted submarine war backed by two hundred to three hundred of these vessels, they would have forced their will on Great Britain before the middle of the following year, and America would have been left completely out of the picture. In fact, like ourselves in the Gallipoli campaign, if they had not prematurely shown their naval claws, they might, in spite of the stalemate on land, have ended the war victoriously by the use of sea power. To-day, if we close our eyes to this fact and attempt to banish the submarine by incantations on the lines of the Declarations of Paris or London, we may, at some day in the

7*

future, suddenly open them to find starvation staring us in the face.

If we examine the basic ideas underlying this whole period of fighting, we shall find, as was the case in all former wars, that killing was the supreme object. Soldiers have killed soldiers since times immemorial; consequently, killing, which is but a means of enforcing the will of one nation on another, has monopolized the whole horizon of warfare. The submarine taught the civilized nations of the world that there were other means of compelling a nation to accept the will of its adversary, and, though its use resulted in men and even women and children being killed, the numbers destroyed were insignificant when compared to the numbers killed by traditional methods. Thus, we come to the conclusion that it was not the killing of non-combatants which was the real crime, for in modern warfare it is pure sophistry to attempt to draw a line between those who fight and those who assist the fighters, since entire nations go to war. Instead, that it was the novelty of the means, in spite of their low killing power, which horrified those who were attacked; for, not having grown accustomed to these means, they were not prepared to defend themselves against them.

Nearly all new methods of waging war have, in the past, humanized the art. Thus, the most brutal form of warfare is axe warfare, the hand-to-hand struggle which ends in the extermination of one side. Musket warfare humanized axe warfare, and, in the last great war, the submarine, aeroplane, gas and tank humanized that condition of warfare which, by 1914, had grown into a traditional art.

A novel weapon or means of warfare, like an unknown plague, fills the imagination of man with horror and intangible fear. Yet, no remedy to this is to be obtained by locking up terror in a mental dungeon; in place, the unknown must be examined in broad daylight, its nature diagnosed and its antidote discovered.

The underlying factor throughout the whole of this period of the economic attack was that, as the fighting forces are maintained by the country to which they belong, they can under modern conditions, be attacked indirectly by the delivery of a direct attack on the nation itself. Siege warfare nearly always demands a costly process of attrition, and never more so than when an entire nation has to be besieged and starved into submission. In the next Chapter I will show that, towards the end of the Great War, a more economical method of attack was taking form, a method which in the future may compel an entire nation to throw up its hands and crave peace within a few days, possibly hours, of a war being declared.

V

THE FIRST LAP OF THE MORAL EPOCH

IN the last Chapter I examined the traditional aspect of the Great War and the main phases which out-cropped from it. I pointed out, as far as space would allow, that the theory underlying the war was that of enforcing policy by destruction of life and of property. The question may now be asked, if this theory is fundamentally unsound, how comes it that it has prevailed since times immemorable? The answer is not difficult to arrive at, when it is realized that national wars, in their modern aspect, are but correlatives of modern civilization, which, since the introduction of steam-power, especially in the form of the steamship and locomotive, has been completely revolutionized. With the adoption of steam as a motive force, we see simultaneously introduced a physical world contraction and an intellectual world expansion. While, in 1750, it took three weeks to travel from Caithness to London, to-day Bombay, Cape Town, San Francisco and Vladivostock can be reached in a similar time. Intellectually, what did this mean? It meant that, as space shrank, intelligence expanded through travel and rapidity of communication. In 1759, the news of the capture of Quebec took several weeks before it was received in London; yet, in 1921, the result of the Carpentier-Dempsey fight was announced to the whole of Paris within three minutes of the knock-out blow being delivered!

This intellectual and moral revolution, which was brought about through a growth in the physical sciences, was not grasped by the military mind. It was not realized that, while only a

hundred years ago, it took days and weeks and months before
a moral blow could be delivered, to-day it only takes minutes
and hours. It was not realized that, while in the year 1800,
the nervous system of a civilized nation was of a low and gang-
lionic order, by 1900 it had become highly sensitive and central-
ized. It was not realized that, as the whole aspect of civilization
had changed, so also must the whole aspect of warfare be changed,
and, as science had accomplished the civil changes, so also must
science accomplish the military ones.

In 1914, what happened was this : unless the war could be
won within a few weeks of its outbreak, armies, as then organized,
could not, under probable circumstances, maintain or enforce
the peace policies of their respective governments, because these
armies, in constitution, belonged to a social epoch which was dead
and gone. For over a hundred years civilization had been built
upon science and steam-power, yet, in 1914, armies were still
organized on muscle-power, the power upon which nations had
been constituted prior to the advent of the steam-engine, the
dynamo and the petrol-engine, the telegraph and the telephone.
As the main target in war—the will of the nation—grew in size
through intellectual expansion and sensitiveness, so do we see,
in order to protect these targets, armies becoming, not more
intelligent and more scientific, but more brutal, ton upon ton of
human flesh being added, until war strengths are reckoned in
millions in place of thousands of men.

This idea of human tonnage was a veritable hallucination,
which became apparent when, in August, 1914, the first machine
gun sent its bullets zip-zipping over the battlefield. This
hallucination, thereupon, began to volatilize, for the soldier,
however well he may have been trained, always remains a creature
controlled by his instinct of self-preservation. What did this
instinct do ? For the next four years, at first unconsciously,
then more and more consciously, it urged the soldier to make good
his hundred years of scientific neglect. Invention was thereupon
piled upon invention, but the killing theory still held the field,
until towards the close of the war it became apparent to some

that science was so powerful that it could even dispense with the age-old custom of killing and could do something far more effective—it could petrify the human mind with fear. It could, in fact, directly dictate the will of one nation to another, and with vastly reduced bloodshed. It could, in fact, enforce policy with far less detriment to the eventual peace than had ever been possible before. The idea of the moral shock, in place of the physical assault, was just beginning to flutter over the blood-soaked battlefields when the Armistice of November 11, 1918, brought hostilities to a close. Since that date this idea has been reduced from a dynamic force to a mere kinetic energy, by solemn international ignorance of the meaning and object of war. In 1921, at Washington, the aim of the Disarmament Conference was to restrict the outbreak of war and to render warfare less brutal, yet the action taken there, as I shall prove, was to render wars more likely and to maintain armies on a footing which, when the next great war engulfs society, will once again demand its million tons of flesh. I will now return to the war of 1914–1918.

If we examine the history of siege warfare, we shall soon discover that the causes of surrender, in order of importance, have been : treachery, starvation and assault. Here we obtain three different means of accomplishing a siege—the attack on the moral of the defenders, the attack on the resources of the defenders and the attack on the defences of the defenders. I have already dealt with the second and third of these means, I will now examine the first.

I will first inquire into the meaning of treachery as applied to war, for it is an ugly word* and its unenviable reputation may, in the minds of some, obliterate its tremendous power. Treachery is a violation of allegiance, the highest form of which is the co-operation of the individuals composing a nation in the maintenance of the nation's free existence. For an individual, who shares in common with others the prosperity of the nation to which

---

* An American writer defines strategy as follows : " When practised by Indians it is called treachery "—which is very true.

he belongs, to refuse, for some selfish reason, to secure the nation against the aggression of an enemy, is an act of treachery. All acts of war ultimately aim at creating a state of treachery in an enemy; in other words, their object is to reduce the enemy's moral to so low a point that he is willing to set aside his national existence or policy, and accept the will of his adversary. Treachery, in its military meaning, is demoralization, and, if we once get the nasty taste of the word out of our mouths, we shall realize that, if by inducing a state of faithlessness or demoralization in an enemy we can more speedily win a war than by force of arms or starvation, we have every right to use treachery as a weapon. By this I do not mean that we should behave like barbarians, or that we should fire at an enemy under a flag of truce, or promise him terms of surrender we have no intention of carrying out; but that to attack the will of the enemy's army and his civil population by a rapid means is quite as honourable an act of war as to attack it by a slow means, such as shooting down his soldiers, sinking his ships and starving his women and children.

I will now examine this question from a very simple standpoint. In a besieged town or fortress, what human elements within it have, in the past, proved the most receptive to treachery? Undoubtedly the civil elements. The reason for this is self-apparent; soldiers are controlled by discipline, civilians by fear. Consequently, the main targets of the moral attack are the civil inhabitants of the country attacked, for if their will can be corrupted, however well disciplined may their soldiers and sailors be, their organization will become affected by the general rot which has undermined the stability of their government. A nation septic with revolution can no more wage an organized war than can a man, contorted with colic, shoot snipe. This was the lesson which Russia taught Europe in 1917, and yet, at that time, the Allied press was unanimous in pronouncing the revolution to be a glorious war-winning event!

On the declaration of war, in August, 1914, the moral attack opened like a labour conference; the contending newspapers collected dirt from the gutters of their respective Fleet Streets and threw it into each other's faces. Later on in the war, the journalists were drilled into some form of order, and well-organized paper attacks were launched, treachery finding its extreme limit in the fictitious and comic discovery of the German Corpse Factories. Curious to relate that, though the power of the press, as a means of demoralization, was fully realized by the British Government, its enormous power to moralize the British Nation was never made use of. Being completely cut off from the realities of war by a short-sighted censorship, the press was never able to bring the people into touch with these realities and, consequently, into contact with their true responsibilities. The people being thus rendered inarticulate, the government was unable to ascertain the popular sentiment on any great question, and when a crisis had to be faced, not knowing how the nation might take it, decision was obscured by ambiguous action, which always permitted of numerous lines of retirement should eventually the people object. What the politicians never realized was that, during war time, the supreme duty of government is to take the nation into their full confidence; for, when national existence is at stake, popular opinion (intuition) is nearly always healthy and virile. The medium between the government and the people, and between the people and the nation's army, fleet, and air force, is the daily press; during the war, this medium, in place of being rendered fluid, was solidified by the chill blast of political fear.

Besides the newspaper-attack, the propitiation of neutrals was extensively made use of as a means of undermining the moral of the enemy's government. Looking back on the results, it is very doubtful whether this diplomatic attack did more damage to the enemy or to ourselves. The reason was that the government relied more on cajolery than on outspokenness. British diplomatic action in Turkey, Bulgaria and Greece, during 1914, was a grotesque failure, and there can be little doubt that, during the period which preceded America's entry into the war, the government was quite as concerned with pleasing the United States as with beating Germany. In place of winning over the Americans—a virile nation—by frankness, this action, though it may have flattered President Wilson, withheld from the people of that great country the seriousness of the Allies' position in Europe. This want of straight talking undoubtedly lengthened the war. What no government appeared to realize, and Germany least of all, was that the poles of the magnet which attract all neutrals worth attracting are straight-fighting and straight-speaking, and why? Because the winners of the war will, in the peace which must one day follow it, exert more control over neutrals than the losers; consequently, it was to the future advantage of the world that the "cleanest" nations should win.

Besides the purely civil means of attacking the moral of a nation I will now turn to the military means. In traditional warfare, it was the rule that armies attacked armies and not non-combatants. If this tradition were strictly adhered to, then the demoralization of the enemy could only be effected by the destruction of the enemy's army and fleet. This process proved a most bloody one, and, during the war, adherence to it resulted in appalling slaughter. It should here be once again remembered that the more bloodless a war is, the more prosperous and contented will the peace, which follows the war, be for all concerned. For example, if, during the recent war, Germany could have been forced to disband her army and scrap her navy by a sudden and enormous loss of national moral, which entailed little bloodshed and small damage to her industries, would not the world to-day be a more prosperous and contented habitation for man than it actually is? There can be no two answers to this question. And, supposing even if this sudden blow had cost the lives of a few thousand German women and children, would this loss have rendered this novel type of warfare immoral? Certainly, if the killing of men is to be considered moral while the killing of women and children, under all circumstances, is an immoral act. The colossal fallacy of this argument is to be sought in the fact that traditional warfare will persistently and blindly think of killing or not-killing as objectives in war. When, however, it is realized that to enforce a policy, and not to kill, is the objective, and that the policy of a nation, though maintained and enforced by her sailors and soldiers, is not fashioned by them, but by the civil population, surely, then, if a few civilians get killed in the struggle they have nothing to complain of—" *dulce et decorum est pro patria mori.*" And, if they will not accept these words as their motto, then, in my opinion, their governments should altogether abstain from war, however much they may be spat upon.

Morality is not a fixed quantity, it is not a law of Nature, but a dynamic and invigorating social force. It, again, is not an end in itself, but a means towards an end—peaceful national survival. Slaughter is the negation of survival; consequently, as the incidence of slaughter is reduced, the more moral, in the natural meaning of the word, does warfare become.

I will now examine certain means of warfare which were used during the Great War, the future developments of which, I believe, will, while minimizing bloodshed and ruin, prove adequate in order to enforce policy.

Nearly all new inventions in war, and not a few in industry, have been attributed to his Satanic Majesty, who must, indeed, be the greatest of all inventors, but, curious to relate, eventually all these inventions have made warfare more and more humane and less and less frequent. If this progress continue, it is quite conceivable that from the week-end wars of the Middle Ages, we may, in the future, expect wars once a century, once every two centuries, until warfare, as we know it to-day, is looked upon as a kind of international cannibalism and nations lose their taste for blood.

When warfare was very simple in nature, the soldier shot arrows at his antagonist; later on he fired cannon balls, and as these played terrible havoc when they bounded through close masses of troops, consequently the infantry opened their ranks in order to avoid destruction. This rather disconcerted the gunner, so he invented the shell and the shrapnel howitzer, and, when the opposing infantry found out, as they did very early in the Great War, that it was useless to open the ranks any further, they dug trenches and went to earth. Once again was the gunner disconcerted, and, while he was attempting to dig the infantry out of their trenches by means of shells, a very expensive operation, a cunning German, following on the lines proposed by Lord Dundonald in 1854, replaced steel particles by gas particles, so that a whole area and all the targets included in it, either above ground or beneath, might be hit.

On April 22, 1915, the Germans put this idea into practice east of Ypres, and inaugurated a mode of warfare which I believe is destined to revolutionize the whole art. They made, however, two cardinal mistakes: first, they used lethal gas—chlorine, which was totally unnecessary, especially so as the Hague Convention did not forbid the use of gases of a non-toxic nature; secondly, they did not use sufficient of it for the winning of a decisive battle. Had they really understood the meaning of gas they could have won the war.

The effects, though restricted, were immediate and appalling, the French and British troops fell back gasping for breath. They could do nothing else, for all their peace training and equipment were useless against this new death. Consequently, tradition was shocked to the marrow, and, without thought, the whole civilized world shuddered with horror, and gas, like gunpowder, chloroform and the locomotive, was pronounced to be the invention of the Devil.

The horrors of gas warfare have been so well advertised that the very enthusiasm shown by its execrators should make us pause and think. What are the facts? The main fact, as regards the brutality of this type of warfare, is to be discovered in the casualty lists. As regards their own losses, the American General Staff have carefully categorized them; they are as follows:

The total number of casualties resulting from all causes

was 274,217. Of these 74,779, or 27.3 per cent., were due to gas. Of the gas casualties only 1,400, or 1.87 per cent., resulted in death. Of the remaining 199,438 casualties, resulting from bullets, shell fire, etc., 46,659, or 23.4 per cent., proved fatal. Here, then, are the facts regarding these alleged horrors. Well may the compilers of this report conclude it by saying :

> "In other words, gas is twelve times as humane as bullets and high explosives. That is to say, if a man gets gassed on the battlefield he has twelve times as many chances to get well as if he is struck by bullets and high explosives."

Further than this, the permanent injuries resulting from gas-wounding are far less numerous than those inflicted by the use of traditional weapons. At the Meeting of the British Association of 1919, Brigadier-General H. Hartley, an expert chemist, said :

> "The death-rate among gas casualties was much lower than that among casualties of other causes, and not only was the death-rate lower, but a much smaller proportion of the injured suffered any permanent disability. There is no comparison between the permanent damage caused by gas, and the suffering caused to those who were maimed and blinded by shell and rifle-fire.* It is now generally admitted that in the later stages of the war many military objects could be attained with less suffering by using gas than by any other means."

I have already stated, more than once, that killing is not the objective in war. If this statement be accepted, then, as

---

* Pacifists and adherents of the traditional war school have deliberately attempted to discredit chemical warfare by stating that gas has blinded thousands of men and affected tens of thousands with tuberculosis. The facts of the case are as follows :

    (i.) Blinding. During the war the Americans had eighty-six men totally blinded, forty-four partially blinded and six hundred and forty-four blinded in one eye. Of the gassed patients four were blinded in both eyes and twenty-five in one eye.

    (ii.) In the year 1918 there were one and a half times as many cases of tuberculosis per thousand among all American troops in France as there were amongst those gassed. In 1919 there were more than one and three-quarter times as many tuberculosis cases per thousand among all troops as there were among the gassed.

        The Report of the Surgeon-General U.S.A. Army, 1920.

bloodshed is uneconomical, surely an attempt should be made to devise a means of forcing an enemy to change his policy by bloodlessly defeating his army. Gas warfare enables us to do this, for there is no reason why gases as weapons should be of a lethal nature. In the last war they were frequently so, because soldiers and the civil suppliers of soldiers had become so accustomed to think in terms of killing, that, when gas was proposed as a weapon, they at once looked upon gas in the form of a microscopic bullet.

On July 12, 1917, at the third battle of Ypres, the Germans gave up this idea, and, by making use of a chemical commonly known as mustard gas, disclosed to the whole world the future possibilities of gas warfare. Respirators to a great extent were now useless, for the persistent and vesicant nature of this chemical rendered whole areas, for days on end, uninhabitable and dangerous to cross. Men carried the oily liquid on their clothes, on the mud of their boots, and infected dug-outs, billets and rest camps far back on the lines of communication. Few died, but many were incapacitated for months on end. Here, curious to relate, is the true power of gas as a weapon—*it can incapacitate without killing*. A dead man says nothing, and, when once buried, is no encumbrance to the survivors. A wounded man will spread the wildest of rumours, will exaggerate dangers, foster panic, and requires the attention of others to heal him—until he dies or is cured, he is a military encumbrance and a demoralizing agent. Gas, as I will show later on, is, *par excellence*, the weapon of demoralization, and, as it can terrorize without necessarily killing, it, more than any other known weapon, can enforce economically the policy of one nation on another. I will now turn to air warfare.

For military purposes the aeroplane had been made use of before the advent of the Great War, both in Mexico and Tripoli, but it was only during the Great War that, in spite of traditional jealousy its immense powers became manifest. At first a mere adjunct to the older services on land and sea, within three years it won its independence, for not only could it hop over armies and fleets and attack the brains of these forces, but it could attack the moral of the government defended by these forces, and, above all, the will of the nation upon which the power of government is founded.

The Germans were, I believe, the first of the belligerents to bombard an open town from the air, and such action, being a novelty, met with universal execration. Nevertheless, it was not long before the Allies retaliated in what was known as baby-killing, but which in truth was the direct attack on the source of all military power—the nerves and will of the civil population.

As it cannot be more immoral to bomb a town than to bombard it, does the immorality of an aeroplane attack lie in the fact that, while in a bombardment the slaughter of women and children is but an unfortunate incident, in an aerial attack on a town the terrorization of its *civil* inhabitants becomes the main object ? I believe that this is the popular conception, simply because civilians have not yet grasped the fact that : when *nations go to war the entire population of each country concerned is ranged against the other,* and that the solidarity of their fighting forces is founded on the civil will. The justifiableness of such attacks was clearly pointed out by Mr. Lanchester as long ago as 1915, when he wrote :

> "It is futile to attempt to disguise the self-evident fact that a serious attack on the capital city of an enemy, containing in its heart the administrative centre both of his Army and Navy, in addition to the headquarters of his Government, cannot be regarded other than as a legitimate act of war. No international agreement or contention can make it otherwise. . . . There is really no escape from this. Unquestionably the destruction of a capital city, such as London, with the administrative centres aforesaid, would be a military achievement of the first order of magnitude ; it would be, from an enemy standpoint, an achievement of far greater potential value than any ordinary success or victory on the field of battle."*

Apparent as this fact is, it was only towards the end of the Great War that the various belligerents began to realize what an attack on the social nerve-centres really meant. Simultaneously,

* " Aircraft and Warfare," F. W. Lanchester, p. 192.

they also learnt that the body of an army attacked by low flying aeroplanes was all but helpless.   In Palestine and Syria the routed Turks suffered seriously from this form of attack, so also did the retiring Austrians in Italy.   Of the last-mentioned operations, Major-General the Hon. S. F. Gathorne-Hardy gives a graphic description in Vol. III., No. 1, of the " Army Quarterly." He says :

> " On these two days (October 29th, 30th, 1918), the Conegliano-Pordonone road was black with columns of all arms hurrying eastwards. On these the few British squadrons poured 30,000 rounds of S.A.A. and three and a half tons of bombs from low altitude. Subsequent examination of the road almost forced the observer to the conclusion that this form of warfare should be forbidden in the future."

Such advice as this is worse than useless, for difficulties are not banished by words, and, if such action were possible, either mankind would become a race of gods or all progress would cease. Curious to relate, a very similar suggestion was made by Baron de Jomini, who wrote his " Art of War " about one hundred years ago.   He says :

> " The means of destruction are approaching perfection with frightful rapidity. The Congreve rockets, the effect and direction of which it is said the Austrians can now regulate. The shrapnel howitzers, which throw a stream of canister as far as the range of a bullet—the Perkins steam guns, which vomit forth as many balls as a battalion—will multiply the chances of destruction, as though the hecatombs of Eylau, Borodino, Leipsic and Waterloo were not sufficient to decimate the European races.
> " If governments do not combine in a congress to proscribe these inventions of destruction, there will be no course left but to make the half of any army consist of cavalry with cuirasses, in order to capture with great rapidity these machines ; and the infantry, even, will be obliged to resume its armour of the Middle Ages, without which a battalion will be destroyed before engaging the enemy.
> " We may then see again the famous men-at-arms all covered with armour, and horses will require the same protection."

His prevision was right, comity of nations could do nothing ; common-sense could do much, and his armoured man materialized in 1916 in the form of the tank, yet another invention which I will now examine.

For many years before the outbreak of the Great War the line along which tactical power was sought was fire, more fire and yet more fire. Protection, except by fire and by extensions, that is by reduction in the size of the target, had been neglected, and increased means of mobility, except for the railway, had scarcely been considered at all. In 1914 (and for all that still to-day), the marching-power of the soldier was about the same as it was in the days of Cheops and Sennacherib.

As the type of fire aimed at was rifle-fire, and as it was well known that a rifle bullet could be rendered perfectly harmless by about 8 mm. of armour, it is truly astonishing, when to-day we look back on the problem, that, before the outbreak of the war, no single soldier of note thought of using the petrol engine and chain track for the purpose of carrying armour in order to protect infantry. The problem is in nature so simple and so self-apparent, that the only answer to the question why then was it not thought of, must be that a tradition, when it becomes fixed in the mind of man, exercises a hypnotic influence over even the most intelligent, and over the less intelligent it is mentally a soporific drug and the most dangerous " dope " of all. So we find that, since 1870, the entire General Staffs in the world had been walking in their sleep. Then suddenly, in August, 1914, they woke up to discover that they were standing outside on the window-sill of a house forty-four stories high—the house of traditional warfare. Fire-supremacy, the very instrument of victory which, for forty-four years, they had been creating, drove friend and foe like rats to earth. Then a common-sense man—Colonel E. D. Swinton—came forward and suggested the tank, and the British War Office refused it !

Thanks to Mr. Winston Churchill, who, in 1914, was First Lord of the Admiralty, the first tanks were produced and, on September 15, 1916, they experienced their baptism of fire on the battlefield of the Somme. At once the British General Staff gave orders for the cancellation of all further production of tanks, but thanks to Sir Albert Stern this order was rescinded. From this date on to the battle of Hamel, on July 4, 1918, tanks had to fight for their existence, not against the enemy's opposition but against tradition, and so well did they fight that, in 1921, General Von Zwehl was able to write : " It was not the genius of Marshal Foch that defeated us, but ' General Tank.' "*

I do not intend here to prove this assertion, for it has already been proved in many books ; in place I will simply take the tank as it existed during the Great War and show that in proportion as it was a life-saving invention so also was it a demoralizing agent, and, further, how it was on the point of revolutionizing tactics when the Armistice put an end to the war.

On the battlefield of the Somme, in 1916, it accomplished little of a startling nature and yet sufficient to have persuaded all but the traditionally blind that it was a weapon wherewith the war on land could be won at comparatively small cost. On September 25, one tank, followed closely by infantry, moved along about a mile of trench line and forced 362 Germans to surrender and at a cost to the infantry of five men killed and wounded. The point to note in this small operation is that the tank was in front of the infantry, a very common-sense position, for just as a man equipped with a shield carries it in front of him and not behind him, so when armoured machines accompany infantry their proper place is *in front !*

Common-sense has, however, nothing whatever to do with tradition ; for, as the tank operations which followed proved, common-sense is generally the antithesis of custom. Because the manuals laid it down that infantry were the decisive arm, and because officers had been fed on the manuals, in spite of the armoured tank, the infantry continued from September, 1916, to November, 1917, to lead the assault. Then, on November 20, at the battle of Cambrai, tradition received such a blow between the eyes that even the most pessimistic asserted that the tank had at length come into its own. At this battle, an advance of 10,000 yards was made in twelve hours at a cost of 6,000 casualties, and 8,000 Germans and 100 guns were captured. At the third battle of Ypres a similar penetration took three months and cost over

* " Die Schlachten im Sommer, 1918, an der West Front," von H. Von Zwehl, General der Infanterie a D.

350,000 casualties.   The traditional school was, however, only tank-shocked.   In April, 1918, the Tank Corps was reduced from 18 to 12 Battalions because infantry reinforcements were falling short!   On July 4, 1918, at the battle of Hamel, tanks started once again *in rear* of the infantry!   The infantry attack was on the point of petering out when the 60 tanks co-operating caught up the leading wave of Australians and led them through to their final objective.   The tank crews suffered no fatal casualties, the Australians lost 672 in killed and wounded and 1,500 Germans were captured.   Then followed the battles of Soissons, July 18, and of Amiens, August 8, and the tank became the terror of Germany.   On July 1, 1916, the first day of the battle of the Somme, the British Army suffered 40,000 casualties; on the first day of the battle of Amiens the casualties were slightly under 1,000 !

During July, August, September, October and November, 1916, the British Army lost approximately 475,000 men, it captured 30,000 prisoners and occupied some 90 square miles of country.   During the same months, in 1917, the losses were 370,000, the prisoners captured were 25,000, and the ground occupied was about 45 square miles.   In July, August, September, October and November, 1918, the losses were 345,000, the prisoners captured 176,000, and the ground occupied was 4,000 square miles. If now we divide these losses by the number of square miles captured, we shall obtain a rough estimate of casualties per square mile gained.   These figures are approximately as follows :

(a) July to November, 1916 :
     $475,000 \div 90$ sq. miles $= 5,277$ casualties per sq. mile.
(b) July to November, 1917 :
     $370,000 \div 45$ sq. miles $= 8,222$ casualties per sq. mile.
(c) July to November, 1918 :
     $345,000 \div 4,000$ sq. miles $= 86$ casualties per sq. mile.

In the third period alone were tanks used efficiently.

During the early days of the third battle of Ypres, in 1917, it became apparent to the General Staff of the British Tank Corps that, though it was always possible, granted the ground was passable, to break an enemy's front by means of tanks, by traditional methods of warfare it was most difficult to prevent this broken front falling back on its reserves or to prevent the reserves reinforcing the shattered fragments. A project was, consequently, devised to overcome this difficulty. It consisted in the use of two types of tanks, one type, 26 feet long, to assault the enemy's front, and another type, 30 feet long, to move right through this front and deposit in rear of it a chain of machine-gun posts· Each long tank, besides its crew, was to carry forward within it 20 machine gunners with 4 machine guns. The point of interest in this novel form of attack was that its target was the *morally weakest point* in the enemy's battle body, namely, his rear.

On May 24, 1918, the General Staff of the Tank Corps made out another project, which carried the attack on the enemy's moral a step further.

From 1914 onwards, traditional warfare had sought to overcome the enemy's resistance by defeating his fighting troops. Such a defeat would result in the demoralization of his command and his administrative services. The demoralization of his command would react on the will of the enemy's people, who might be reduced to so nervous a condition that they would either overthrow their government or force it to sue for peace. As the means of this method of warfare were superiority of weapon-power and man-power, that is brute force, and as, in the spring of 1918, the Germans were numerically superior to the Allies, there appeared no immediate chance of winning the war by traditional methods. Consequently, it was considered that some other solution should be attempted. The proposals made were as follows :

The strength of the enemy's fighting forces depended on the solidarity of their organization, which, in its turn, rested on the integrity of the enemy's command and system of supply. If these two props could be knocked away, then the whole of the battle front supported by them would collapse. In order to effect this *moral débâcle* of the enemy's body, the Tank Corps

General Staff suggested that, for the 1919 campaign, two separate forces of tanks should be employed :

   (i.) A force of fast moving machines which, under cover of darkness or smoke, would, at top speed, rush through the enemy's fighting body and, making for all Divisional, Corps and Army Headquarters, paralyse these brain and nerve centres by direct attack ; simultaneously, other fast machines were to attack all railheads, supply and signal centres, and reduce the personnel at these points to a state of panic.

   (ii.) A force of slower and more heavily armoured machines were to precede the attacking infantry and assault the enemy's front at the moment the faster machines were demoralizing and destroying the brains and stomach.

It was considered that if an attack of this nature could be delivered on a frontage of from 80 to 160 kilometres, such a demoralizing blow would be delivered that the greater part of the German front in France would crumble and produce such a condition of despair within Germany that the Germans would accept defeat.

The operation was a novel one, and it redounds to the credit of the Imperial General Staff in London that they accepted it in detail, and on July 20, 1918, communicated it to Marshal Foch, then Generalissimo of the Allied Armies, who agreed " in every way with the main principles of the study." Consequently this plan of operations was accepted as the basic tactical idea for the 1919 campaign.

Though Fate was to decide that this attack was not to take place, since hostilities terminated in November, 1918, it is nevertheless interesting to note the following evolution : that the war opened with traditional warfare ; that the underlying idea of all traditional operations is killing ; that by degrees this idea gave way to that of demoralizing, until, finally, a method of attack was devised which all but ignored brute force and which for slaughter substituted nervous shock, aiming a moral blow at the brain in place of a physical blow at the body of the enemy's army.

VI

THE WEAPON OF THE FUTURE

IN the last Chapter I showed that the tactical tendency in modern warfare was to strike at the moral rather than at the muscle of an enemy; I also stated that, in my opinion, gas would prove itself to be the weapon which, of all weapons, could accomplish this blow the most economically. The tank and aeroplane, be it well remembered, are not weapons, but only vehicles—means of carrying weapons.

In this present Chapter I intend examining gas as a weapon. First of all it should be realized that the utility of gas in war is not a new idea. In modern times, this idea was thought of in 1812 and again during the Crimean war by Lord Dundonald. In 1864, Mr. B. W. Richardson, considering gas warfare, went so far as to write:

> " The question is, shall these things be ? I do not see that humanity should revolt, for would it not be better to destroy a host in Regent's Park by making the men fall as in a mystical sleep, than to let down on them another host to break their bones, tear their limbs asunder and gouge out their entrails with three-cornered pikes; leaving a vast majority undead and writhing for hours in torments of the damned ? "*

In 1899, the employment of lethal gas as a weapon was discussed at the Hague, and its use was forbidden, this prohibition only serving to give Germany, in 1915, a superior weapon to those wielded by her enemies. Possessing no protection against it, the British and French troops suffered accordingly, and anathematized the new weapon, not only because it was new,

* *Popular Science Review*, 3.176. (1864).

but because it was extremely powerful and Germany held
the whip hand as regards its production. The evil name then
given to gas has, in the popular imagination, clung to it ever
since, for the people do not reason, because what their eyes
have read their lips repeat. With the populace I have no quarrel,
for they are docile, thoughtless creatures depending on others
for their ideas ; but with people like Sir Edward Thorpe,
President of the British Association in 1921, it is otherwise,
for they at least are presumed to be intelligent. Following
in the footsteps of the worthy Baron de Jomini, some of whose
ideas I have already quoted, Sir Edward has pronounced the
use of lethal gas to be " one of the most bestial episodes in the
history of the Great War. . . . Surely," he exclaims, " comity
among nations should be adequate to arrest it " and then,
deviating from the path of Jomini, the only means he suggests
is to leave the solution of this problem to the unfortunate
League of Nations, and to urge all scientists to set their face
" against the continued degradation of science in . . . augment-
ing the horrors of war ! " Gas warfare is not, as Sir Edward
Thorpe asserts, " the very negation of civilization," for it is,
in fact, a product of civilization and an outcrop of science which
will endure ; because, as Captain Auld says :

> " Chemical Warfare has come to stay. It is inconceivable that
> the light barriers of mutual consent or of edict can effectively close
> the road I speak of. Military history and human nature are against
> it at every turn. No case is known of a successful new weapon or
> a tactical advantage having been discarded once its value was ap-
> parent. No agreement or treaty has proved strong enough to bind
> an unscrupulous enemy seeking an advantage, or for that matter
> one with its existence at stake. To avoid the new road is to risk
> being passed in the race of preparation and being outflanked and
> overwhelmed in the event of hostilities.
> " Whatever we do in the matter we can bind no one but ourselves.
> Until war ceases we must be prepared. Apathy is suicidal. Prejudice
> is a crime."*

There can be no doubt, outside Bedlam, of the wisdom

* " Chemical Warfare," by Capt. S. J. M. Auld, O.B.E., M.C., *Royal Engineers Journal*, Feb., 1922.

of these words, just as there can be no doubt that the decision of the Hague Convention presented Germany, a country unscrupulous and fighting for her life, with a means wherewith, had she been wise, she might well have won the war. Yet, at the Washington Disarmament Conference of 1921, at which were assembled intelligent human beings, what do we find was decided ? As follows :

> " The use in war of asphyxiating, poisonous or other gases, and all analogous liquids, materials or devices, having been justly condemned by the general opinion of the civilized world and a prohibition of such use having been declared in Treaties to which a majority of the civilized Powers are parties;
>
> " The Signatory Powers, to the end that this prohibition shall be universally accepted as a part of international law binding alike the conscience and practice of nations, declare their assent to such prohibition, agree to be bound thereby as between themselves and invite all other civilized nations to adhere thereto."

Then, in place of defining what is meant by " all analogous liquids, materials or devices," a veritable witches' cauldron of mysteries, this Conference, in the footsteps of Sir Edward Thorpe and others, indulges in abuse. The Report continues :

> " It undertakes further to denounce the use of poisonous gases and chemicals in war, as they were used to the horror of all civilization in the war of 1914-1918.
>
> " Cynics have said that in the stress of war these rules will be violated. Cynics are always near-sighted, and oft and usual the decisive facts lie beyond the range of their vision."

Before I examine the first part of this astonishing agreement, I will examine the question of the cynics :

Giordano Bruno died at the stake because he was a cynic. Galileo perished in prison and Copernicus just died in time to escape persecution because they were cynics. Roger Bacon, a terrible cynic, hid the secret of gunpowder in a cryptograph. Solomon de Caus was locked up in a madhouse for proclaiming that ships and vehicles could be moved by steam. Simpson, who first made use of chloroform in obstetrics, was considered an agent of the devil, and so was Jenner, the introducer of vaccination against smallpox. George Stephenson, probably the greatest

of all cynics, was virtually outlawed. His invention, the locomotive, was declared to be " contrary to the law of God," because " it would prevent cows grazing, hens laying, and would
cause ladies to give premature birth to children at the sight of
these things going forward at the rate of four and a half miles
an hour ! "

With reference to the locomotive, I cannot forbear quoting
from the *Quarterly Review* of 1825, for the quotation is in
character so traditional.

> " What can be more palpably absurd and ridiculous than the
> prospect held out of locomotives travelling TWICE AS FAST as stage
> coaches ! We should as soon expect the people of Woolwich to
> suffer themselves to be fired off upon one of Congreve's ricochet
> rockets as trust themselves to the mercy of such a machine going
> at such a rate. We will back old Father Thames against the Woolwich
> Railway for any sum. We trust that Parliament will, in all railways
> it may sanction, limit the speed to EIGHT or NINE MILES AN HOUR,
> which, we entirely agree with Mr. Sylvester, is as great as can be
> ventured on with safety."

Gunpowder, the most revolutionary military discovery
prior to that of gas, was anathematized beyond belief. In the
Middle Ages wars were very frequent, because weapons were
very simple and unscientific. Knights boasted of their courts
and codes of chivalry, but, when battles took place, there was
usually, as one chronicler puts it, " a horrid slaughter among
the common folk." The reason for this was that the common
folk were not worth taking prisoners—they had little in their
pockets. Then came Roger Bacon's gunpowder, and, as Carlyle
says : " this logic even the Hyperborean understands," for,
" it makes all men alike tall. . . . Hereby, at last, is the
Goliath powerless and the David resistless ; savage animalism
is nothing, inventive spiritualism is all." Mind has in fact
triumphed over body, and upon gunpowder is modern democracy
founded.

Needless to say, the knight, who, dressed in steel plate, was
immune from democratic sticks and stones, strongly objected
to be shot by a poltroon, that is, a peasant armed with an

arquebus. To give such a knave power over the knight was an insult which could not be tolerated; it was utterly barbarous, and as late as 1626 we find a certain Mr. Monro writing :

> " It is thought that the invention of cannons was found first at Nuremberg for the ruin of man . . . how soone the trumpet did sounde, the enemy was thundered on, first with those as with showers of hailstones, so that the enemies were cruelly affrighted with them, men of valour being suddenly taken away, who before were wont to fight valiantly and long with the sword and lance, more for the honour of victory ; than for any desire of shedding of blood ; but now, men are marterysed and cut downe, at more than half a mile of distance, by these furious and thundering engines of great cannon, that sometimes shoote fiery bullets able to burn whole cities, castles, houses or bridges, where they chance to light, and if they happen to light within walls, or amongst a briggad of foote or horse, as they did at Leipsigh, in the grave fon Torne his briggad, spoiled a number at once, as doubtless the devilish invention did within Walestine, his leaguer at this time."

Mr. Monro was wrong, because gunpowder humanized sword and lance warfare. The cynic of 1626 was right, and so, in 1922, will the cynic once again prove himself right, because gas will humanize the type of warfare Monro objected to, but which the members of the Washington Conference wish to maintain. Just as William Napier objected to the introduction into the British Army of the Minié rifle, a weapon with a range of one thousand yards, because, as he said with some heat, " it would turn infantry into long-range assassins," so, to-day, do we find many eminent people objecting to gas warfare, because, being a novelty, its meaning is only sufficiently understood by them to realize that it may disturb their preconceived ideas, which, through long acquaintance, have become cherished personal belongings.

I will now turn back to the compact and examine the peculiarly ambiguous wording—" other gases and all analogous liquids, materials or devices." What do these words mean ? They vaguely and all embracingly can mean nothing outside everything. In fact they mean that no chemical whatever may be used in war. This is absurd, because no nation can accept a decision which excludes all harmless lachrymators and smokes which may save life, as well as high explosives which give off carbon monoxide. If this compact be carried to its ultimate conclusion, then the use of petrol gas in military motor cars, and of coal gas in officers' billets, are also forbidden ! The above words exclude and debar so much that they really include nothing, for all that an enemy has got to do, in peace time, is to prepare vast quantities of various gases, for he knows for a certainty, from the wording of this compact, that innumerable excuses will always be found on the battlefield, such as the use by his adversary of T.N.T. or picric acid, which will provide him with an excuse to retaliate with the real " stuff." " To us," to quote from an American scientific journal, " the endeavour to abolish chemical warfare throughout the world by the resolutions of the present Conference reminds us of the experience of King Canute in commanding the tides not to rise." Personally, it reminds me of that " cunning " bird the ostrich.

I will now inquire into the military reasons why I believe that gas will prove itself to be the weapon of the future.

First of all what is a weapon ? A weapon is a means of imposing by force a policy upon an adversary. The policy of a nation, as I have explained, should be enforced with the least loss possible to either side and to the world at large. The less this loss the better will the policy enforced flourish. The security of peaceful prosperity is the object of war, not slaughter. A weapon should, therefore, possess the following characteristics :

(i.) Its production should not detrimentally affect prosperity.
(ii.) It should be simple to manufacture in peace or war.
(iii.) Its nature should be unknown to the enemy.
(iv.) It should economize time on the battlefield.
(v.) It should incapacitate without killing.
(vi.) It should permit of an antidote being known to the side using it.
(vii.) It should effect no permanent damage to property.

The weapons of traditional warfare do not permit of these characteristics being developed, as they are all based on the idea of physical and material destruction. Gunpowder revolutionized the means of war but not its underlying idea, and it only gave rise to the use of more powerful weapons of the killing type; and so all the more frightening and, consequently, less destructive. I will now show that gas as a weapon will not only effect an equally great revolution of means, but also a revolution in idea.

(i.) *Economy in Production.* Armies and navies are of necessity expensive organizations, because they detract in place of adding to peaceful prosperity. During the last hundred years they have become more and more costly in proportion as the means used by them have diverged from the civil means. At the beginning of the last century a good fowling-piece differed little from the musket of the day, and a merchantman could rapidly be converted into a ship of war. To-day the rifle and machine gun have no civil uses outside Ireland, and a super-Dreadnought not only possesses no commercial value, but detracts from commercial prosperity by costing about £8,000,000, or considerably more than the whole British Navy did in 1823.

Gas is an article of commerce, and most of the gases employed during the Great War were manufactured not only by the normal commercial processes but from chemicals in everyday use. Modern civilization could scarcely exist if such chemicals as chlorine, phosgene and hydrocyanic acid were removed. Thousands of tons of all these substances are yearly made use of for bleaching, disinfecting, dyeing and killing rodent and insect pests. Consequently, we see that, in gases and war chemicals, we possess not only a means of securing national prosperity, but also a means of fostering it. This in itself constitutes a stupendous economic revolution. To-day, Germany possesses seventy per cent. of the organic chemical output of the entire world. In the next war she can use, if she so will, the whole of her chemical plant for the production of warlike chemicals. Great Britain possesses but eleven per cent. of the world's output. What does this mean? It means that, in spite of the treaty of Versailles, which limited the size of Germany's army, navy, and air force, Germany still possesses gas supremacy, and, of this supremacy in 1915, Mr. Balfour, at the Washington Conference, said that, " the result had been very near to a complete disaster for the allied armies." Should not we, therefore, do our utmost to foster organic chemistry at home; yet how can we create the necessary supply unless we create a demand for it. If gas becomes our predominant weapon, then a demand for it will be created, and in seeking for new war gases we shall undoubtedly discover chemicals of great commercial utility. " The Chemical Warfare Service," says Mr. R. S. McBride, " furnishing as it does an important link in the chain of chemical industries, contributes to peace-time welfare of the community." This alone sufficiently justifies its cost, " even though its military value as a measure of defence were entirely ignored."*

Compared to the cost of the means employed in traditional warfare, the cost of war chemicals is insignificant. On January 16, 1922, in a speech before the Compressed Gas Manufacturers' Association, New York City, Brigadier-General Amos A. Fries, chief of the U.S.A. Chemical Warfare Service, said :

> " Chemical Warfare cost the United States in the World War just about $150,000,000. The total cost of that war to the United States is estimated at $30,000,000,000, or two hundred times the cost of Chemical Warfare, and yet Chemical Warfare had a profound influence in causing the Germans to surrender. Briefly, Chemical Warfare was as cheap as it was effective and humane. If the United States wants economy in peace while at the same time being prepared for any emergency, gas is the weapon above all others."

(ii.) *Simplicity of Manufacture.* Simplicity of manufacture of weapons during war time is frequently a synonym of victory. Men are generally forthcoming, but unless weapons can rapidly be produced in bulk these men are useless, and, unless the nature of the weapons made is simple, bulk production will not be rapid. During the recent war, the training of the British New Armies was seriously delayed on account of shortage of weapons, and it was not until the beginning of 1918, or after more than

* " Chemical Warfare and the Arms Treaty," R. S. McBride, *Chemical and Metallurgical Engineering,* February 22, 1922.

three years' strenuous effort, that sufficient shells were produced to satisfy the demands made. If, before the war, we had devoted our attention to war gases, it is quite conceivable that we might have discovered a gas against which the Germans would have possessed no immediate protection, and that, by firing a few thousand projectiles loaded with this gas from the existing field guns, we should have attained greater results than we did by multiplying high explosive shells by the million ; which, in their turn, demanded thousands of extra guns and gunners to fire them. During the war, we multiplied the nature of our guns and so complicated training. What gas enables us to do is to use the same gun and only change the nature of the chemical inside the shell, which scarcely, if at all, affects the training of the gunners. Further still, gas is, what may be called, a universal weapon ; that is to say, " in the mechanics of firing chemical ammunition there is no difference whatever from the mechanics of firing high explosives or shrapnel."

For any weapon to be manufactured rapidly, it is necessary to have its components at hand. If a country cannot produce these, then at any crisis it may suffer from a weapon-famine. What is the main source of chemical warfare ? Coal—coal-tar and oil, from which also most of the medicines and dyes of the world are produced. In Great Britain we possess vast resources of coal ; consequently, for chemical warfare supplies we are not dependent on foreign products. Not only is it unnecessary for us to obtain from abroad our raw material for weapons, but, in place of spending our money on foreign nitrates, we can spend it on home-mined coal. Germany is also a great coal producing country ; if in another war, as in the last, she loses her command of the sea, is it humanly likely that she will placidly accept defeat because of a shortage of traditional weapons when gigantic resources for the production of chemical weapons are actually but a few yards under her feet ?

(iii.) *Secrecy of Nature.* Secrecy in the nature of weapons is the foundation of tactical surprise, and surprise, as I have shown, is the most economical principle whereon to build grand tactics. In war, surprise is the pivot of victory. In the past, the brute-force theory of warfare has to a great extent been foisted on to the armies and navies of civilized nations on account of their inability to keep their weapons secret. And, when they have attempted to do so, as in the case of the French mitrailleuse in 1870, training has suffered so severely that on the battlefield the weapons have proved useless. The difficulty has been, and still is, that once a weapon is in the hand of the soldier its characteristics soon become known to other nations, the most noted exception to this being the recoil system of the French 75 mm. field gun. In this case, however, it was unnecessary for the soldier to examine it, yet once in the hands of the soldier this contrivance might easily have been sold to a foreign country.

It is not practically possible to keep a bullet or a shell secret. It is, however, possible to keep the contents of a shell secret. A new explosive may be discovered and may be kept secret, but in effect it will only be a modification of existing means of destruction. A new gas may, however, be kept an absolute secret, and, what is equally important, its antidote may be kept secret as well. During peace time, let us suppose that a gunner is trained to fire shells filled with chlorine gas and that the container of his respirator possesses the necessary antidotes to chlorine. On mobilization he is given shell X and he changes his training respirator for one possessing substance Y, which is an antidote to X. X and Y are absolute secrets, he has not the faintest idea what they are, and yet they may enable him to defeat his adversary within a few minutes of the first attack being launched. I will corroborate this self-evident advantage possessed by chemical weapons by again quoting from Mr. McBride.

> "Gas as a military agency can be developed by research and its manufacture continued in secret indefinitely, if any nation wishes, despite any number of international agreements to the contrary. In this respect it differs fundamentally from battleships and fortifications, which cannot be so secretly constructed and preserved."

(iv.) *Economy of Time*. The activities of war, even more so than those of peace, are controlled by time, for in war speed and improvisation are predominant conditions. As regards weapons, time, in its military sense, is a correlative of effect. Thus, the speed of fire, such as is possessed by the machine gun, would be useless if the bullets were ineffective, and ineffective they frequently are when fired against an earthwork, or a tank, or into the blue. With gas the actual rate of fire may be much slower than that of traditional projectiles, though as it is normally carried within these projectiles, it is the same. But, if volume of fire be considered, it will at once become apparent that no traditional weapon possesses this quality to the extent of gas. From a rifle ten aimed shots can be fired in a minute, from a machine gun six hundred, from a field gun twenty shells, and, if shrapnel, each will contain 365 bullets, so that in a minute 7,300 bullets will be fired. Gas is, however, composed of chemical molecules each of which can disable ; consequently, the projectiles of a gas bombardment cannot be reckoned by thousands per minute but by thousands of trillions. In fact, so immense a number, that it is not even necessary to know the position of the target ; all that is necessary is to know in what area it is, and then to inundate this area. Unlike a bullet, the effect of gas does not cease once the force generated to propel it is spent, for, while the bullet is " dead " the gas molecule is " alive," and may remain alive for days after gas has been projected. If the reader can imagine a machine gun which can fire millions of bullets a second, each bullet drifting on after the force of the original discharge has been spent, creeping through trees and houses, wandering over walls and into shelters and dug-outs, then he will have some idea how gas can be used to economize military time.

(v.) *Economy of Life.* I have already repeatedly accentuated the fact that, in modern warfare, the object is to enforce a policy and not to kill and destroy. I realize that, in all probability, for many years to come killing will be an unavoidable attribute of battle, but it stands to reason that, if killing can be reduced, warfare will become more economical and the object of war will be the better attained. I have already examined the alleged horrors of gas warfare and have shown definitely that, during the recent war, it was twelve times as humane as traditional warfare. In my opinion it can be made more humane still directly the idea of killing is replaced by that of incapacitating. A bullet is essentially a lethal weapon, for it is impossible to design a non-lethal bullet which would be of any practical use in war. It is, however, quite as feasible to employ non-lethal gases as lethal ones, and their power to incapacitate is enormous. During the third battle of Ypres, General Fries states, " that the British had over 160,000 gas casualties, but only 4,000 deaths—2½ per cent." Whether these figures are correct I am unable to say, but, as a partaker in this battle, I can vouch that after mud, mustard gas was the severest resistant encountered.

On the three days preceding the attack, on March 21, 1918, it is estimated that the Germans fired 250,000 mustard-gas shells against the British Third Army, which suffered a loss of 500 officer casualties.

> " In spite of the fact that the Germans had no reserve gas for many days after the beginning of the Argonne fighting—the greatest battle in American history—the gas casualties among the Americans, according to the best information, amounted to 27.2 per cent. of all American battle casualties. This is all the more remarkable when we consider that about one half of all American battle casualties occurred in the battle of the Argonne, where the Germans had practically no gas. They had used up all reserves of that material against the British and the French earlier in the season, and hence had only daily production to draw upon."[*]

These are a few examples of the direct effect of gas as an incapacitating weapon; I will now examine its indirect effect. If soldiers, in order to protect themselves against bullets, had to don armour, even if this armour could be made proof, the bullet would not lose its whole value, for, by forcing the soldier to wear armour, it would soon reduce him to a state of physical exhaustion. In place of attacking his body it would attack his mobility. Gas, by compelling a soldier to wear a respirator, can accomplish this important military result. " Physical vigour," writes General Sibert (Director Chemical Warfare Service, U.S.A., in 1919), " is

[*] Extract from United States War Department Annual Report, 1919.

9*

one of the greatest assets in any army. Gas, used properly and in quantities that will be easily obtainable in future wars, will make the wearing of the mask a continuous affair for all troops within two to five miles of the front line, and in certain places for many miles beyond. If it never killed a man, the reduction in physical vigour and, therefore, efficiency of an army forced at all times to wear masks would amount to at least 25 per cent."

If the statistics of the total casualties of the Great War, so far as they are ascertainable, are examined, it will be found that by far the greatest number of casualties were suffered by the infantry, and that these casualties were inflicted by infantry weapons—bullets fired by rifles and machine guns. It follows, consequently, that, if infantry could be abolished, warfare would be made much more humane and economical than it is to-day, and, as one writer puts it, " without infantry, the ravages of war would be reduced something like eighty per cent.," and then adds, " When the frock coats get about the long table and begin to talk about limiting war's barbarity, they want to realize that they won't do much good by omitting a little of the millinery of war. What the world wants them to do is to keep the infantry at home."*

Gas will accomplish this very effectively, as I will now show.

An infantry soldier cannot go into action in a diver's suit with a mile or two of piping played out from a spool on his back, yet so powerful are certain modern gases, such as Lewisite, that they will penetrate without difficulty all ordinary clothing and burn the skin beneath it. To put a man into an air-tight suit is impracticable, as in battle he will die of heat apoplexy. Infantry, as infantry, can play but a small part in gas warfare, and with their disappearance can war be humanized, as I will show later on.

There are two further reasons why gas warfare will economize life by reducing casualties. The first is that, as I have explained, gas is a universal weapon, it can be used by all arms ; consequently, the result will be what I will call a universal type of casualty. The nature of all wounds will be very similar, because the means of inflicting them will be similar ; consequently, medical

* *Racine, Wisconsin, Call,* January 7, 1922.

arrangements on the battlefield can be simplified. The second is that, since new war gases can be kept secret, surprise in war will become more frequent and, consequently, the winning of victories will be speeded up. The shorter the war the less, normally, is the loss resulting.

(vi.) *Assurance of an Antidote.* In traditional warfare the only universal antidote to being killed is to kill, hence its barbarous and blood-thirsty nature. From time to time means have been sought to reduce casualties—such as body armour, helmets, shields and entrenchments. Gas is, however, unlike all traditional weapons in that, if a new gas is discovered, immediately an antidote can be provided for it. Consequently, it is now possible to send men into battle equipped with weapons against which the enemy may possess no protection, while our own men are completely protected. This in itself constitutes such a colossal tactical revolution that it is difficult at present to see where it will lead. In my own opinion it will sound the death-knell of infantry as we know them to-day, and how this will be accomplished I will explain in a future Chapter. One fact requires, however, to be accentuated, namely, no nation can hope to protect their fighting forces effectively against gas unless offensive gas warfare is studied during peace time and the troops themselves trained to understand what this form of warfare entails.

(vii.) *Economy of Property.* As the objective in war is to guarantee and safeguard prosperity, destruction, even of the enemy's property, should be avoided. In modern warfare the means of destruction have become so great that no nation considers its frontiers safe unless it possesses an army sufficiently powerful to destroy the enemy before the enemy can destroy it. The horror of the results of invasion was one of the causes not only of the Great War but of the armed peace which preceded its outbreak.

The war of 1914-1918 was a war of high explosives, and traditional methods of destruction were carried to such a pitch that entire towns were demolished, villages completely vanished, not a stone remaining, and the surface of hundreds of square miles of fields, vineyards and orchards was literally blown away. It is incredible that anyone, who has the welfare of humanity at heart, can wish to repeat this devastation. Yet it cannot be avoided as long as traditional warfare is maintained. Substitute gas warfare for high explosive warfare and a remedy presents itself; this is what the short-sighted cynic wants, but the professional humanitarian will have none of it. Why? Because he is blinded by tradition, and should he happen to be a politician, he is unable to forget his votes—truth must be obscured so that he may continue to rule the blotting-paper brained multitudes.

After reading through what I have already written, I cannot conceive how any rational person can have the face to maintain that traditional warfare is more economical and humane than chemical warfare. I can understand anyone wishing to abolish war, for the world is full of those who have no stomach for a fight ; but I cannot understand how it is possible for people judged sane, people who have lived through the last war, even if at a safe distance, wishing to repeat its destruction. This they are doing as long as they prevent armies and fleets developing on scientific lines. For the prosperity of the world, scientific military research is essential. "Scientists are making," says General Hartley, " very rapid advances, and many of these will have a direct bearing on the next war. It is absolutely essential to make adequate provision to continue research on gas warfare problems, as otherwise all preparations for defence may prove valueless. . . . Such research can only be made effective by the closest sympathy and co-operation between soldiers and scientists, and unless their co-operation is much closer than it was before the late war, there will be little chance of success. It is for the scientists to explore the possibilities and to develop such as are thought likely to be of value, and for the soldiers to apply the results to their investigation of war problems."*

At least a military generation will have to pass by before a stock of soldiers is bred which can fulfil their part in this contract,

* " British and German Gas Warfare," Brig.-General H. Hartley, C.B.E., M.C., *The Journal of the Royal Artillery*, February, 1920.

and then it will take another generation of soldiers to work out scientifically the changes which traditional tactics must undergo. Those of us who believe in the inevitability of war are nevertheless apt to think, as great wars only occur at about fifty year intervals, that, whatever changes science may demand, we have ample time to rest before seriously setting to work to discover what the next great war will require. No assumption could be more fallacious, for, before a new military idea is accepted, a whole school of obsolete ideas, religious in their intolerance, has to be converted to the new idea, and not until it is converted will efficient training take place, and training is an all essential of victory. If the truth must be known, should the next great war explode in 1972, then, if we work hard, we may just be able to convert the traditional school in time and replace it by a school of military scientists. Not brawny halberdiers skilled at the game of push of pikes or push of bullets or push of shells, bullets and shells which strike down fool and sage alike ; but intelligent thinkers who will push their ideas to the detriment of the enemy's beef, who will pit brain against muscle, and, if opposed by muscle alone, will win a war quite possibly in a night without a day, as in the next Chapter I will explain.

VII

THE FUTURE OF AIR WARFARE

IN the last Chapter I stated that gas was a universal weapon because it could be employed by all types of arms. In this Chapter and the two following, I will substantiate this statement by showing that to-day we are approaching the adoption of a universal means of military movement which will more completely than ever before enable the universal weapon to be employed.

In the past, the motive force of all military movement on land has been muscular power, and, tactically, this was the main motive energy used throughout the Great War, which, in my opinion, will definitely close a military epoch stretching from the cave man to the present day. This muscular power was of two degrees—human and animal. Tactically, the soldier is simply a weapon mounting of about one-eighth h.p. energy, which limits, to a considerable extent, the nature and power of the weapons he carries. In the past, in order to increase the speed of the soldier the only means available was to mount him on an animal of greater muscular energy than himself, and if, when so mounted, he was unable to carry a certain weapon, this weapon was either carried on an animal or hauled by one or more animals. In the South African War we see as many as thirty-two oxen harnessed to a five-inch gun, and each animal requiring fodder added enormously to the complexity of war.

As the limitations of muscular energy in their turn limited the nature and power of weapons, consequently we see, especially in modern times, the introduction of a great variety of weapons, each attempting to make good certain deficiencies in the others due to the deficiencies in their mountings. Thus, for example : if it were possible for an infantryman to carry a machine gun and several thousand rounds of ammunition, the rifle would long ago have been scrapped. And, again, if it were possible for six horses to haul at high speed a six-inch gun and one hundred shells, eighteen-pounder field guns would no longer be required. But such changes have not been possible because muscle power possesses definite limits.

To-day, we possess an all but universal means of movement —the petrol engine, which will influence land weapons as it is to-day influencing air weapons, and as steam has and is influencing naval weapons. At sea, in capital ships, we see a tendency towards a universal weapon—the big shell ; and in auxiliary craft a tendency towards a universal weapon— the torpedo. These weapons are very similar in nature, though the first is used for out-fighting and the second for in-fighting, for both are but metal containers filled with high explosives.

In the air there is a greater difference, two entirely different weapons being used. The big aeroplane carries the bomb and the small the machine gun. In the future, I believe that these two weapons will more closely coincide ; this I will discuss presently ; meanwhile, I will examine the most universal means of movement yet devised, namely, the aeroplane, with its power of movement in three dimensions.

Though the power of three dimensional movement by aircraft is generally recognized, the influence of this power on the future of warfare is in continual dispute, because, so I believe, we have not yet learnt to think of war from its third dimensional aspect.

Hitherto strategy, or the art of moving fighting units—armies or fleets—has been either one or two dimensional in nature. On land, the major strategical movements are normally one dimensional, because armies, and particularly modern armies, cannot move or supply themselves rapidly unless movement is directed along roads, railways, canals, or rivers. These constitute *lines* of advance, each line possessing two directions, that is facility to move forwards or backwards. Where these lines do not exist, the nature of war tends towards that of partisan operations; in other words, wars in countries devoid of communications are tactically small wars, however large the forces employed may be. At sea, naval movements are in nature two dimensional, because the vehicle of movement is an *area* and not a line; the exception to this rule is the power of movement of the submarine, which I will discuss in Chapter IX.

Bearing in mind these three dimensions of movement, it will at once be recognized that the future strategical problems of war are closely connected with the protection of land roads, sea roads, and air roads, in order that trade may prosper, and, in the event of it being threatened, may be secured by military force.

As the powers of aircraft include the dimensions of movement made use of by armies and fleets, it stands to reason that, of the three great defence forces of civilized nations, the air force is the only one which can closely and continually co-operate with the other two. On account of this ability to co-operate, that is to move with armies or navies and yet independently of them, we are faced by the following portentous strategical problem : may not this power of aerial co-operation become so perfect that, in place of aircraft co-operating with navies and armies, these forces will instead co-operate with aircraft, and that possibly, at some date in the future, the utility of armies and navies will be reduced to zero, aircraft entirely replacing them ? I will shortly examine this problem, which embraces the following three sub-problems :

(i.) The influence of aircraft on land warfare.
(ii.) The influence of aircraft on sea warfare.
(iii.) The independent action of aircraft in air warfare.

Before examining these sub-problems, it is necessary to make certain of the tactical limitations of aircraft, for this will enable us to consider these problems logically.

Aircraft are of two types—the lighter and the heavier than air machines. I am of opinion that the main purpose of the airship in future warfare will be the carriage of supplies rather than offensive action, though these vessels may assist this action by long-range reconnaissance. The airship is virtually the tramp steamer of the air, and there is no reason why vessels should not be built which could circumnavigate the globe, or carry a hundred tons and upwards for distances ranging over thousands of miles. Compared to an aeroplane, the airship is a slow moving craft with a lower ceiling on account of the danger of rising above the hail line; it is conspicuous even at high altitudes, readily picked up by searchlights and easily held within their rays. It is easily attackable and cannot well be armoured, it requires a numerous personnel to maintain it, an expensive housing and mooring system, and it is a gluttonous consumer of gas. Its one predominant characteristic is that it can remain motionless in the air without the expenditure of energy.

The chief characteristic of the aeroplane is speed of locomotion in three dimensions. This speed to-day is well over 150 miles an hour, and, when diving, 300 miles an hour further still, many aeroplanes can climb at 1,000 feet the minute. When in movement, an aeroplane can proceed straight from point to point, motion in the air encountering no physical obstruction as on land and sea. Its predominant limitation is that it cannot remain motionless in the air, to which may be added that the ceiling of a useful war machine is unlikely to exceed 30,000 feet.

From the above we may deduce the elements of its tactical nature—a high offensive power and limited means of direct protection, that is protection by armour. The greater its radius of action the less offensive it becomes on account of petrol replacing armament, and the more it is protected by armour the less will be its range of action on account of steel replacing petrol. From these deductions, I will extract three tactical requirements which later on I shall refer to, namely:

(i.) Aircraft protection is to be sought for in the height they can operate from the ground.

(ii.) Aircraft offensive power, if the above protection is to be maintained, depends on the size of the target.

(iii.) Aircraft radius of action depends not only on the amount of petrol, etc., carried, but on refilling while in the air.

Bearing in mind the aeroplane's three dimensional power of movement and that the air presents to it no physical obstacle, the size of an air force is, in theory, unlimited. In practice, however, this is not true, for as aeroplanes cannot remain motionless in the air, the factor which limits the numbers which can usefully be employed is landing ground, which is more and more difficult to find as aeroplanes increase in size.

Besides this limitation, the following are of secondary importance : it becomes readily " bogged " in a ground mist, sense of direction is frequently lost in cloud and fog, landing at night and in foggy weather on unprepared landing grounds is dangerous, and further, though an aeroplane is not tied down to definite tracts of country, as wheeled vehicles are, or to definite expanses of water, as ships are, it is to a very considerable extent tied down to its landing grounds. In the Great War, on account of its static nature, no great difficulty was experienced in providing these ; nevertheless, in France during the last eighteen months of the war, the average wastage in aeroplanes was between fifty and eighty per cent. per month. Of these casualties but one quarter were due to hostile action, the greater number resulting from crashes on landing. Will crashes in future be less frequent ? This is doubtful in spite of improvements to be expected. Consequently, as belligerents may have to replace their entire equipment of machines once every two months, either an immense number of reserve machines will have to be maintained during peace time, or co-operation with the slow moving land forces abandoned, or a plan of attack evolved which will decide the war within a few weeks or days or hours of its outbreak.

I will now turn to the three problems of this Chapter :

The Influence of Aircraft on Land Warfare.—At present we

do not posses a tactical theory of aerial warfare. Our outlook during the recent war, and to a very great extent to-day, was and is a Homeric one. Hero met hero in hand-to-hand fight, and victories were based on individual contests. From this primitive type of warfare we must expect in the future to see evolve an elaborate tactics, for in the next great war capture of the air will become of supreme importance, because of all tactical " positions " the air is the one which commands all others. Once this supreme point of vantage is gained, the next tactical operation will be to deliver an aerial attack on the land forces, not only on their bodies—their men, horses and guns, but on their brains—their command headquarters ; on their nerves— their system of communications ; on their internal organs— their bases, supply depots, chemical and engineering works and workshops.

The ultra-traditional school does not hold these views ; its adherents possess little if any imagination, and what was good enough for the army and navy in 1914 is good enough for these forces to-day. Such is the opinion which they hold, in spite of the fact that armies and navies as organized and equipped in 1914 *did not* win the war. But to these bats blinded by light this is the fault of the war and not of the 1914 organization. Their ignorance is colossal and is only excelled by their lack of vision. On Armistice Day, 1918, a typical adherent, without a smile on his face, said to me : " Thank God ! we can now get back to real soldiering." Aircraft are quite useful in order to assist the other arms, to range their guns and to fly about with cameras and bombs ; they can co-operate, of course ; but act independently—never ! As to replacing infantry or Dreadnoughts—absurd ! Such are the views held by the older and fruitier traditional vintage.

The new and raw wine, still not quite fermented, thinks otherwise. It realizes that the aeroplane is a new means of waging war, and it applies it to the old end—killing and destruction. Consequently, in place of humanizing war and so rendering it less costly and wasteful, these thinkers are frequently terrified by their own thoughts. What do they see? They see columns of foot and horse wending their way towards their battle area, whole divisions twelve miles long toiling along dusty roads. Then they see in the distance tiny specks on the horizon, they grow bigger, there is a droning of engines—twenty low flying armoured battle planes top the rise in front, and, before the wretched infantry have time to unstrap their limbered vehicles and mount their machine guns, there is a rattle of musketry from twenty times twenty machine guns. In ten minutes the whole column is traversed from van to rear, 250,000 bullets have been pumped into it—not 30,000, as on the Conegliano-Pordonone road—and the very dust of the highway is churned into a porridge of blood.

Such warfare as this is truly horrible, because it is so one-sided. To shoot down infantry in this manner is mere massacre. But such slaughter must continue so long as infantry exist and so long as tactics are controlled by the traditional school. Further, this school believes in material destruction. In the aeroplane they behold a means of accentuating destruction to such an extent that killing in bulk will become unnecessary. Here at least we see a glimmer of light, economic destruction replacing the killing of human beings. Of this type of attack Mr. Lanchester writes :

> " Depots of every kind in the rear of the enemy's lines would cease to exist ; rolling stock and mechanical transport would be destroyed ; no bridge would be allowed to stand for 24 hours ; railway junctions would be subject to continuous bombardment. . . . In this manner a virtually impassable zone would be created in the rear of the enemy's defences, a zone varying, perhaps, from 100 to 200 miles in width . . . not only will the defence be slowly strangled from the uncertainty and lack of supplies of all kinds, but ultimately retreat will become impossible. The defending force will find itself literally in a state of siege under the worst possible conditions. . . . Thus, in the extended employment of aircraft, we have the means at hand of compelling a bloodless victory."*

I do not intend to waste my ink in proving that the old vintage is wrong. To all beings, possessed of any intelligence,

* " Aircraft in Warfare," Lanchester, pp. 187, 188.

this must be apparent. Instead, I intend showing that though the new wine of war is perfectly right in asserting that aeroplanes can destroy infantry like vermin, and devastate whole districts, it is extremely foolish to use such means of imposing the will of one nation on another, when non-lethal gases will enable this same end to be attained with incomparably greater economy of life and property.

Let us picture to ourselves again the infantry toiling along the road. The aeroplanes approach; they do not skim a hundred feet above the road, but fly at an altitude well outside effective bullet range. They open their chemical tanks and a fine spray and fog envelopes the astonished column of men. Suppose that this gas is a deadly poison, all these men will shortly die; such an end is anyhow better than being shot to pieces. Suppose this gas is a vesicant chemical, like mustard gas, all these men will be wounded and only one per cent. *may* die. Cruel though such an attack is, it is incomparably better than being shot to pieces, and, if not killed, probably maimed for life. Suppose that this gas is but an anæsthetic, then the whole column will fall, as Richardson poetically wrote in 1864, " into a mystic sleep," and when its twenty thousand men awake, if they do not find themselves prisoners, they will have anyhow lost several good marching hours. What general on earth is going to win decisive battles, battles which need the most careful assembly and speedy concentration of troops, if whole divisions and army corps are going to be put to bed for several hours at a time, two or three times a day? Consequently, traditional infantry, the greatest slaughterers of all, have no place on the future battlefield, not because they are harmless but because they are absurd! And with them must depart cavalry and all horse-drawn guns and vehicles; in fact, the whole of the traditional army of 1914 will have become a phantom.

I will now turn to Mr. Lanchester's picture. Why drive the car of Juggernaut over entire areas? Why destroy depots, bridges, railways and workshops in order to strangle, bloodlessly though it may be, the enemy's troops which are in advance of them ? Even to-day a depot drenched with a sneezing mixture would cease to fulfil its duties, and a mile of roadway or railway drenched with a strong lachrymator would become impassable for days on end. More impassable than if the road were smothered in barbed wire or the rails removed from the permanent way. Why destroy, when no one really wants to destroy ? When I ask Mr. Jones to sign an agreement, I do not knife him if he refuses, for if I do so he may die, and then his signature, my objective, will be unobtainable. To destroy a nation is to destroy the very objective of peace ; consequently, the less the destruction the more complete to the winner is the victory.

Some time back, I made mention of three tactical requirements, the first of which was that aircraft protection is to be sought for in the height the machines can operate from the ground ; and the second, that the offensive power of aeroplanes depends to a great extent on the size of the target. I will now examine the relative value of machine guns, bombs and gas as aircraft weapons. For a machine gun to be effective the aeroplane must fly low, which means that it must forgo its natural means of protection or hamper its mobility and restrict its offensive power by carrying armour. For a bomb to be effective the target must be sufficiently large to be hit easily ; the higher the aeroplane flies the smaller does the target appear to be. Here we are faced by two difficulties which would seem to be irreconcilable. This is, however, not so, for liquid gas sprayed from a machine or dropped in bombs, which burst in the air like shrapnel, will form a gas cloud which, within certain limits of height, increases in size in direct ratio to the height of the machines from which it is dropped on account of the liquid atomizing as it falls through the air. A bullet or bomb maintains its form until it strikes the target or the ground ; gas acts otherwise, its form increasing in size as it nears the ground ; consequently, a gas attack delivered from a height against a small target is likely to prove a much more effective attack than one made with bullets and bombs. Again, if a high wind is blowing, it is not necessary to aim at the target, but in place to manoeuvre for wind, which an aeroplane can always do, and then drop the gas at a distance from the target and let it drift over it. Yet again, suppose that the traditional arms—infantry, cavalry, and field guns—are strongly protected by anti-aircraft artillery and machine guns and the attacking aeroplanes are afraid to approach them, all that these machines need do is to fly ahead of the hostile column and drench sections of the road it is marching along, preferably defiles and road-junctions, with persistent lethal or non-lethal gasses, which will compel the traditional arms to wear their respirators continuously. What will their rate of march then be, seeing that the infantry carry fifty to sixty pounds of arms and equipment ?

The answer is : at best two or three miles a day, for marching in respirators, especially in hot weather, is not a practical military operation. In my opinion, the fact of the case is that THE TRADITIONAL SOLDIER IS DOOMED.

The Influence of Aircraft on Sea Warfare. I will now turn to the second problem—the influence of aircraft on sea warfare.

I have already accentuated the fact that the main theory of all past naval warfare was that fighting at sea is a two dimensional operation. However, during the recent war, two weapons possessing three dimensional powers came into use—the submarine and the aeroplane (or seaplane). The first caused consternation, and the second proved a useful adjunct for purposes of reconnaissance and observation, but the combined use of these two weapons was not understood. Combined, their offensive power may well prove enormous.

What does the traditional naval attack entail—slaughter in an accentuated form. On land, military units are seldom exterminated, at sea the extermination by drowning of entire ship's crews is the rule and not the exception. Off Coronel, the *Monmouth* and the *Good Hope* went down with the loss of all hands, and, of Admiral von Spee's squadron, very few were saved from the icy waters of the South Atlantic. Of all forms of warfare, sea fighting is the most prodigal ; in ten minutes a ship, costing £8,000,000, manned by 1,250 sailors, may be sent to the bottom. Destruction by maximums is what the naval mind aims at.

Besides a new vintage of soldiers, there is growing up amongst us to-day a new school of sailors ; men who, though they are considering the new means of naval warfare, are still obsessed by the old idea—destruction. They picture a fleet of Super-Dreadnoughts pursued by aeroplanes like bears pursued by bees. High above they swoop and whirl. Thousands of small smoke bombs are loosed into the air, they whistle downwards, strike decks and sea, and a minute later all is lost in an immense cloud of rising smoke. A veritable volcanic eruption has been projected from heaven. Under cover of this cloud and the loss of fighting efficiency caused by every sailor having to wear a respirator, dive down torpedo aircraft, while submarines race over the surface of the water towards their prey. Immense explosions throw into the air great columns of water, and vortices of smoke vibrate upwards. Little by little the smoke clears. Where is that proud fleet ? It is gone : £100,000,000 worth of steel is swirling downwards through the depths below, and the surface of the sea is dotted with thousands of human forms as if they had been shaken out of some giant caster. There are oaths and groans and shrieks ; then, with horrible gurglings, one by one they vanish to join their ships : there is silence and the victory is won !

What a senseless waste of good steel and better human life. What an inane and barbaric attempt to gain more prosperous peace terms than those which existed before the outbreak of hostilities. Why destroy, why not capture ? Here then is another picture.

The fleet of Dreadnoughts is steaming in line ahead, preceded by a cruiser screen. Then again do the aeroplanes approach and the smoke bombs are showered down. They are toxic, and the crews are killed and disabled, but the ships are saved. They are vesicant, and the decks are splashed with mustard gas ; the ships are saved and the crews are mostly disabled. They are filled with a colic-producing chemical, and, as the submarines once again approach, they emit immense clouds of the same irritant. Respirators are adjusted, but the chemical penetrates them as cloud after cloud sweeps over the great vessels. Men groan, they are doubled up, the crews are demented, gun stations are abandoned, discipline is cast to the winds, there is panic and pandemonium, and not a shell or a torpedo is fired. A motor-boat puts out from a submarine and skims over the water towards the enemy's flag ship. A rope ladder is fired into the air, it whirls upwards and its grapnels become engaged with the bridge. A man in a mask swarms up it, to the bridge he goes ; the commander-in-chief is squatting in a corner groaning and holding the pit of his stomach. The man in the mask says : " Hoist the white flag, or the whole of your fleet will be sunk in five minutes ! " Up goes the signal of surrender, and a few days later £100,000,000 worth of steel rides at anchor in a hostile harbour, and thousands of foreign sailors are eating biscuits and bully behind the wire of the prisoners' cages. Not a ship has been lost or damaged, and the casualties have been under five per cent., and most of these were caused by fright and panic.

The question may now well be asked, how can such an operation be carried out in the middle of the Pacific ? The answer is not a difficult one, if the third tactical requirement I laid down is remembered, namely, that the radius of action of aircraft depends on refilling with petrol while in the air, and in this case, also, while on the water.

Aircraft carriers can proceed anywhere a battleship can steam. They will form the sea bases of the air attack, but they possess this disadvantage, that to refill, and especially during battle, aeroplanes will be forced to leave their protective element—the heights of the air, and descend to dangerous altitudes, and eventually to the still more dangerous surface of the sea. Consequently, I believe that airships will be used as air bases, on the envelopes of which aeroplanes can alight to refill and refit at ease. In the future, such moving bases should be able to carry a hundred tons or more of supplies and could, in their turn, replenish their stock from large supply submarines which, possessing power to submerge, would be able, without great danger, to proceed un-escorted to various rendezvous in the oceans and seas in the neighbourhood of the theatre of war.

The Independent Action of Aircraft.   Whether I have solved the two preceding problems I must leave it to the reader to judge.   I have purposely avoided detail, and have merely elaborated an idea which I believe to be possible ; yet, never-theless, I believe both the above problems and the solutions I have outlined to be subordinate to the third problem, which I will now examine.

I have, earlier in this present Chapter, hinted at the possibility that, in the future, air forces may replace armies and navies. Actual replacement is, in my opinion, a misconception of the objective in war. Armies and navies are lethal instruments of security, but the true object, as I have frequently stated, is not to kill soldiers or sink ships, but to change a policy which these soldiers and ships are protecting.   If, in the event of war, an air force can change this policy with less physical destruction than in the past it has been possible to attain by means of armies and navies, and this may be the case, then the air force will not absorb the military purpose of navies and armies, which in nature is tactical, but will instead establish a new conception of war, a conception in which naval and military forces will have either no place at all or one which is subordinate to their present purpose, and by subordinate I mean the occupation of land and sea *after a moral victory has been won on land* by aircraft.

This problem is the most vital military problem of to-day, for, if my supposition be correct, not only will our present-day armies and navies be valueless *in war*, but the immense sums of money spent on them during peace-time will be squandered.

I have already pointed out that the policy of a nation is founded on the will of its civil inhabitants, and that the supreme military power of aircraft is their ability " to hop " over armies and fleets and attack what is in rear of them.   Here then is this vital problem in brief : can a hostile nation be forced to change its will by means of an independent aerial attack ?

That such an attack is possible was visibly demonstrated to all who inhabited Paris and London during the Great War. At first, being in nature a novelty, it was dubbed immoral. Is this assertion, however, true? Only so far as all warfare may be classed as immoral, in which case the less the ethical and economic damage done during a war the more moral will the waging of it become. This leads us to the following question : will aerial warfare in the future, should it supersede land warfare, do more damage than the damage resulting from land warfare as to-day conceived and accepted? I believe that it may, if the object is to obliterate towns and cities by means of high explosive bombs. I believe that it will not, if the nerves of the people are attacked by an offensive directed against their bodies by means of non-lethal gases. I have shown that the statistics of the gas casualties suffered by the American Army during the Great War prove that gas warfare, including the use of deadly gases such as chlorine and phosgene, is twelve times as humane as bullet and shell warfare. Further, I have pointed out that the general assertion that gas warfare is immoral is founded on the fact that nations have not yet realized that great wars are national wars in which the attack on the will of the so-called non-combatants is the objective. Further, I believe that the civilian will fight this idea to the death, because it is far more comfortable to raise forces of men called soldiers and let them slaughter each other, not always to the disadvantage of the civilian, in place of the civilian being attacked directly. In the past such attacks have been difficult to deliver because warfare was two dimensional in nature, and where armies moved (on a plane surface, the crust of the earth) other armies met them and blocked their way. This condition still holds good for armies and navies but not for air forces, and as the object of war is to attack the will of the enemy's people, and as aircraft possess the ability to avoid armies and navies, is an air force going to be so foolish as to attack these forces in place of attacking this will? Whatever the civilian may desire or squeak for, to put it vulgarly, in the next great war he is going to be " in the soup," and what kind of soup will it be? A pretty hot one !

I have pointed out in a former Chapter that destruction can be avoided by the use of non-lethal gases, and that the "political" danger of such chemicals is that they can incapacitate and terrorize without killing.   I believe that, in future warfare, great cities, such as London, will be attacked from the air, and that a fleet of 500 aeroplanes each carrying 500 ten-pound bombs of, let us suppose, mustard gas, might cause 200,000 minor casualties and throw the whole city into panic within half an hour of their arrival. Picture, if you can, what the result will be : London for several days will be one vast raving Bedlam, the hospitals will be stormed, traffic will cease, the homeless will shriek for help, the city will be in pandemonium.   What of the government at Westminster ? It will be swept away by an avalanche of terror.   Then will the enemy dictate his terms, which will be grasped at like a straw by a drowning man.   Thus may a war be won in forty-eight hours and the losses of the winning side may be actually nil !

If a future war can be won at the cost of two or three thousand of the enemy's men, women and children killed, in place of over 1,000,000 men and incidentally several thousands of women and children, as was the case in France during the recent war,* surely an aerial attack is a more humane method than the existing traditional type.   Further, the material damage done will be insignificant when compared to the damage effected during the recent war, the cost of which can only approximately be reckoned in thousands of millions sterling.

Here then is the moral of this Chapter :

In the future, when once the storm clouds of war burst, a nation dare not depend on gaining time wherein to make good its deficiencies in preparation.   In place it must be ready to act, and act at once.   The only arm which can so act, which can mobilize and fight within twenty-four hours of an outrage taking place, is an air force.   This liberty of immediate action is, in fact, its

---

* The total soldiers, sailors and airmen killed during the Great War has been estimated at between nine and ten millions.   The loss among the civil populations, excluding Russia since the close of 1918, due to killed, diseases directly attributable to the war, and fall in birth-rate, has been estimated at twenty millions.

supreme duty, and, however important co-operation with the navy and army may be, first and foremost must an air force be prepared to act alone. The morality of such action is beyond question, for self-preservation is a human right. To commit *felo-de-se* by denying to an air force power of retaliating against the will of the enemy, is the act of a nation which has become insane.

Lightning Source UK Ltd.
Milton Keynes UK
UKHW052251310822
408116UK00014B/569